✶✶✶✶✶✶✶✶✶✶✶✶✶✶✶✶✶

BASEBALL
SUPERSTARS

Ty Cobb

✶✶✶✶✶✶✶✶✶✶✶✶✶✶✶✶✶

✶✶✶✶✶✶✶✶✶✶✶✶✶✶✶✶

Hank Aaron

Ty Cobb

Lou Gehrig

Derek Jeter

Randy Johnson

Mike Piazza

Kirby Puckett

Jackie Robinson

Ichiro Suzuki

Bernie Williams

✶✶✶✶✶✶✶✶✶✶✶✶✶✶✶✶

✳ ✳ ✳ ✳ ✳ ✳ ✳ ✳ ✳ ✳ ✳ ✳ ✳ ✳ ✳ ✳

BASEBALL SUPERSTARS

Ty Cobb

Dennis Abrams

CHELSEA HOUSE
PUBLISHERS

An imprint of Infobase Publishing

✳ ✳ ✳ ✳ ✳ ✳ ✳ ✳ ✳ ✳ ✳ ✳ ✳ ✳ ✳ ✳

TY COBB

Chelsea House
An imprint of Infobase Publishing
132 West 31st Street
New York NY 10001

Library of Congress Cataloging-in-Publication Data
Abrams, Dennis, 1960-
Ty Cobb / Dennis Abrams.
   p. cm.— (Baseball superstars)
Includes bibliographical references and index.
ISBN-13: 978-0-7910-9439-6
ISBN-10: 0-7910-9439-1
1. Cobb, Ty, 1886-1961—Juvenile literature. 2. Baseball players—United States—
Biography—Juvenile literature. I. Title. II. Series.
GV865.C6A27 2007
796.357092—dc22
[B]   2007006222

Series design by Erik Lindstrom
Cover design by Ben Peterson

Printed in the United States of America

Bang EJB 10 9 8 7 6 5 4 3 2 1

This book is printed on acid-free paper.

All links and Web addresses were checked and verified to be correct at the time of publication. Because of the dynamic nature of the Web, some addresses and links may have changed since publication and may no longer be valid.

CONTENTS

Hero Worship

According to the *Compact Oxford English Dictionary*, a hero is a person who is admired for his or her courage or outstanding achievements. Throughout history, people have always had heroes. Sometimes the heroes have been men of legend and myth, like Hercules. The Greek hero Achilles, in the story of the Trojan War, is another example of this kind of hero. Sometimes the heroes have been men of great military achievements. Men like Julius Caesar or Napoleon Bonaparte were regarded as heroes by some for their accomplishments in conquering other countries.

Often, heroes are people we look up to because of their courage in standing up for what is right. Their heroism lies in their efforts to make the world a better place for everyone. These are people like Martin Luther King, Jr., Nelson Mandela,

Eleanor Roosevelt, and Bono. As you can see, heroes may have all different kinds of achievements.

Today, many people become heroes because of their athletic accomplishments. Athletes like Michael Jordan, Tiger Woods, Roger Clemens, Michelle Kwan, Peyton Manning, and Mia Hamm are among today's most admired athletes. Fans look up to them for their strength and grace. They are admired for their competitive drive and for their ability to win. People want to be like them. Their achievements make them role models for young and old alike.

Sports heroes, though, are not a new phenomenon. Just like today, people in years past looked up to the athletes of their own time. Stars from the 1920s, '30s, '40s, and '50s—like Joe DiMaggio, Joe Louis, Babe Ruth, Jackie Robinson, and Babe Didrikson Zaharias—were admired as much by their fans as any of today's stars are. Many of you may have relatives old enough to have seen these sports legends play. They would still remember their greatness and how their fans worshipped them.

THE EARLY GREATS

Very few people are alive today who watched baseball players from the early twentieth century, but players like Honus Wagner, Christy Mathewson, and Tris Speaker were equally admired by fans of their generation. Fans avidly traded their baseball cards and followed their records in the newspapers. They dreamed of playing like them. Perhaps the greatest of these early players, and the man whom many consider to be the greatest baseball player of all time, was Ty Cobb.

Such talk is not exaggeration. As quoted in Al Stump's book *Cobb*, renowned player and manager Casey Stengel said in 1975, "I never saw anyone like Ty Cobb. No one even close to him as the greatest all-time ballplayer. . . . It was like he was superhuman."

Baseball Hall of Famer George Sisler said about him, "The greatness of Ty Cobb was something that had to be seen, and

TY COBB

Ty Cobb, depicted in this 1912 trading card, was perhaps the greatest baseball player of the early twentieth century. Cobb, who played in the major leagues from 1905 to 1928, mostly with Detroit, was known for his hitting skills and his speed around the bases. "The greatness of Ty Cobb was something that had to be seen, and to see him was to remember him forever," said George Sisler, a fellow Hall of Famer.

to see him was to remember him forever." As Joe DiMaggio said, "Every time I hear of this guy again, I wonder how he was possible."

Ty Cobb's achievements as a ballplayer are legendary. Known for his batting ability and speed as a runner, he had no obvious weaknesses as a player. When he retired in 1928, he held 90 major-league records. Many of those records still stand today. He still holds the record for the highest career major-league batting average (.367). He won the most career batting titles (12). He stole home plate more times than anyone who has ever played the game (54).

Cobb's strengths as a batter were unsurpassed. He had an extraordinary eye for the ball. For example, he struck out swinging only twice during the entire 1911 season. He batted over .400 for a season three times in his career. His batting average was .320 or higher for 23 straight seasons. Even in his final season, at the age of 41, his average was .323.

For decades, Cobb held the record for the most career major-league hits, with 4,191. This record stood for nearly 60 years until it was finally broken by Pete Rose in 1985. It is interesting to compare the amount of time Cobb and Rose each took to reach that number. Cobb went to bat 11,429 times, averaging one hit per 2.7270 appearances. To reach the same number of hits, Rose batted 13,763 times, or one hit for every 3.2839 times at bat. If Cobb had batted as many times as Rose, he would have had 5,047 hits. Conversely, if Rose had gone to bat only as often as Cobb, his hit total would have been only 3,480.

With his phenomenal speed, Cobb also held the record for the most career stolen bases with 892. This record, too, was finally broken, first by Lou Brock and then by Rickey Henderson.

In 1936, Cobb became the very first player elected to the new Baseball Hall of Fame. Members of the Baseball Writers' Association of America vote on which players are inducted into the Hall of Fame, and candidates have to be named on 75 percent of the ballots. The maximum number of votes available on that first ballot was 226. Cobb received 222 votes. Honus Wagner and Babe Ruth tied for second place with 215 votes each. They were followed by pitchers Christy Mathewson with 205 votes and Walter Johnson with 189. The

★ ★ ★ ★ ★
NATIONAL BASEBALL HALL OF FAME AND MUSEUM

The National Baseball Hall of Fame and Museum is located at 25 Main Street in Cooperstown, New York. It opened on June 12, 1939.

Do you know why the museum is in Cooperstown, New York? According to legend, Abner Doubleday, who would serve in the Civil War as a Union general, "invented" the game of baseball in Cooperstown in 1839. That is why it was decided to build the Hall of Fame there, in the birthplace of baseball.

Many historians, however, doubt the Abner Doubleday/ Cooperstown story. They point out that games similar to baseball had been played for many years before 1839. And, they say, although Doubleday left many papers and journals, none of them mention baseball.

The museum serves as the center for the study of baseball. It also displays baseball-related artifacts and exhibits. And, the Hall of Fame serves to honor baseball's best players, managers, umpires, and executives.

Exhibits include newspaper articles, uniforms and equipment, photos, baseball cards, films, and plaques honoring Hall of Fame inductees, among others. Since its inception, as of 2007, 280 individuals have been inducted into the Hall of Fame.

A trip to Cooperstown is a must for any true baseball fan. Since its opening, more than 13 million people have visited the hall.

voting demonstrates the huge amount of respect that Cobb had earned as a ballplayer.

NOT ALWAYS HEROIC

It is important to keep in mind that heroes are also human beings. And as human beings, they have their weaknesses and faults. Perfection on the field, or in any kind of endeavor, does not necessarily make someone a perfect person. Indeed, sometimes the very qualities that make someone a great athlete—drive, determination, and a quest to be the best— are often qualities that contribute to their imperfections off the field.

We like to believe that our heroes are special. We sometimes think that, because they are stronger or faster or can hit a baseball better than most other people, they must be superior to us in all ways. That is not the case. Just like everyone else, heroes have their flaws. They are, after all, just people.

Cobb was no exception. He was greatly admired as an athlete. He was equally disliked for his racism and his violent temper. As American writer Ernest Hemingway said about him, "Ty Cobb, the greatest of all ballplayers." But, he added, Cobb was a terrible human being.

Throughout his career, Cobb was accused of being a "dirty" ballplayer, an accusation he always denied. It was said that he would do anything necessary to win. He was particularly disliked (especially by opposing teams and their fans) for his aggressive baserunning and stealing.

He was often accused of intentionally driving his spikes into any fielder who tried to stand between him and the base. It was even said that he purposely sharpened the spikes on his shoes to cause deeper cuts when he drove them into the leg of a shortstop, or first, second, or third baseman—or even the catcher. Cobb always denied the truth of that story.

In his autobiography, he did admit that he would not stand for "being taken advantage of." As he put it,

Ty Cobb took a high slide into the knees of the opposing team's catcher during a game in the 1920s. Cobb had a reputation as a "dirty" player. He denied the accusation and said he was just doing whatever he could to win. Off the field, too, he was known for his violent temper and racist attitudes.

I did retaliate. That I freely admit. If a player took unfair advantage of me, my one thought was to strike back as quickly and effectively as I could and put the fear of God into him. Let the other fellow fire the first shot, and he needed to be on the *qui vive* (on the alert) from then on. For I went looking for him. And when I found him, he usually regretted his act—and rarely repeated it. I commend this procedure to all young players who are of the aggressive type. The results are most satisfactory.

Cobb was also known for his violence off the field. On many occasions, his violent streak got him in trouble with the law. In 1908, for example, while walking down the street in Detroit, he stepped into freshly poured asphalt. He was yelled at by the man pouring the asphalt, Fred Collins, who was African American. Cobb punched Collins, knocking him to the ground. Cobb was charged with assault and received a suspended sentence. He did pay Collins $75 to avoid a civil suit.

Incidents like that one, and worse, continued throughout Cobb's life. Despite his extraordinary success in baseball, he never found a way to control his violent temper. He also never overcame his racism against African Americans. In his mind, he used fighting as a way to defend his "honor," his wife, his team, or anything else he thought was important. Unable to take a joke or laugh at himself, Cobb frequently beat anyone who he felt laughed at or made fun of him.

To Cobb, nothing was more important than the game of baseball. Everything else in his life came in second to his desire to be the best. Through talent, intelligence, determination, and hard work, he did achieve his goal to be the best. His achievements on the field make him worthy of respect and admiration. He was and is a true baseball hero.

But as you will see, the rest of his life was far from heroic. In no way can he be considered a personal role model. Then again, his goal was not to be a role model. He just wanted to play baseball. As Cobb put it, "Baseball was 100 percent of my life."

Childhood

Tyrus "Ty" Raymond Cobb was born on December 18, 1886, in the house that once belonged to his maternal grandmother. The house was located in The Narrows, in Banks County, Georgia.

The Narrows was not an actual town. It was a poor, small community of scattered farms in northeast Georgia. Only about 10 dozen families lived there. There was no railroad, no mayor, and no sheriff.

Ty's father was William Herschel Cobb, who was born in 1863 in Cherokee County, North Carolina, right across the Georgia border. As a child, he left home early, traveling by covered wagon to attend school in Hayesville. He later graduated with first honors from the North Georgia Military

College in Dahlonega. After graduation, he began to work as a schoolteacher.

He was an itinerant, or traveling, schoolteacher. Small communities throughout rural Georgia often had only a one-room schoolhouse. One teacher would serve to teach all grades, from first to twelfth. These rural communities were often very poor. Parents would come together to raise enough money to pay a teacher for a year. Some years, though, the crops would be bad, and in those years, they would often be unable to pay their teacher. The teacher would then be forced to move on to a new community. Through this constant moving, William Cobb met the woman who would become his wife.

Amanda Chitwood was only 12 years old when she married 20-year-old William Cobb. It was uncommon but not rare at that time for girls that young to marry. Gossips said that Amanda was still playing with toys at the time of her marriage.

Three years later, when she was 15 years old, Amanda gave birth to her oldest son, Tyrus, who became known as Ty. One of William Cobb's favorite stories of history was of the ancient Phoenician city of Tyre. In 332 B.C., the residents of the city fought bravely but ultimately lost a battle against the soldiers of Alexander the Great. The name Tyrus was derived from Tyre.

Two years later, Amanda gave birth to another son, John Paul. Four years after that, in 1892, Ty's sister, Florence Leslie, was born.

To begin to understand Ty Cobb, it is important to understand where and when he grew up. The year Tyrus was born, 1886, was only 21 years after the end of the United States Civil War. Georgia had been a part of the Confederacy. It was one of the 11 states that seceded from the United States in 1860–61. In part, the states left the Union to maintain their right to keep African Americans as slaves. After the South was defeated, slavery was banned throughout the United States, and the slaves were freed.

Twenty years after the end of the war, memories were still fresh in the minds of many Southerners. They resented that they had lost the war. They fought it over and over again in discussions with friends, trying to figure out how they could have won.

Both of Ty's grandfathers fought for the Confederacy. It seems quite likely that they told him stories of the war and of what they saw as the correctness of the Southern cause. Cobb also had other relations who made names for themselves during the war. Howell Cobb, who had been the U.S. Treasury secretary before the war, served in the Confederate Provisional Congress and the Confederate Army. T.R.R. Cobb was a brigadier general who died at the Battle of Fredericksburg.

Some people speculate that part of Cobb's angry attitude as a ballplayer was derived from his upbringing after the Civil War. When Cobb broke into baseball, he was one of the few Southerners playing the game at the professional level. The vast majority of players were Northerners, the much hated "Yankees" who had defeated the South in the war.

As teammate Sam Crawford is quoted as saying in Richard Bak's book *Ty Cobb: His Tumultuous Life and Times,* "He came up from the South, you know, and he was still fighting the Civil War. As far as he was concerned, we were all . . . Yankees before he even met us."

Even after the war, many Georgians still believed that African Americans were inferior to whites. Laws were passed that banned black people from voting, holding office, or even going to school with whites. Many Southerners felt that African Americans should always treat whites with respect. They had to address white people as superiors, act in a subservient manner, and refer to them as "sir" or "ma'am." Young Ty learned this attitude at an early age. He carried it with him until the day he died.

For him, upholding the "honor" of the white man was essential. Because of this, Cobb would become angry with any

Howell Cobb, who was one of Ty Cobb's relatives, had been the U.S. Treasury secretary before the Civil War. Then he joined the Confederate Army. Both of Ty's grandfathers also fought for the Confederacy, and when Ty was growing up, memories of the war were fresh in the minds of Southerners. Cobb was one of the few Southerners to play major-league ball in his time, and one teammate said he seemed to still be fighting the Civil War.

African American who he felt spoke back to him or did not treat him with the respect and deference he thought he should receive. That person risked being yelled at or even physically attacked. This behavior, while common in the South, was not as common in the North. So, when he took such actions during his playing days, he often received negative publicity in the press.

SETTLING DOWN

During the first six years of Tyrus's life, the Cobb family was constantly on the move. Going from one teaching position to another, the family lived in Commerce, Lavonia, Carnesville, and Hickory Grove, among other small farming communities in Georgia.

As he described in his autobiography, *My Life in Baseball: The True Record*, Ty's earliest memories were of traveling—"of a buggy, bumping along a red clay road. I seem to recall that I was barefoot and wore a hickory shirt under a pair of bib overalls. With my legs dangling over the tailgate, I was busy winding yarn around a small core ball. It was slow work."

When Tyrus was six or seven, the family finally settled down. His father was offered a position in Royston, Georgia. Though it only had a population of about 500, the town was fairly prosperous. It could afford to support a good school and to pay William Cobb good wages. Soon, he was able to buy a two-story house in town. Later, he bought a 100-acre farm outside of town. There, he raised cotton as well as other crops in the rich Georgia soil. The additional income helped to make him one of the town's more influential citizens.

Tyrus entered into the typical life of a small-town boy. He went to school in the fall, winter, and spring. In the summer, he worked on his father's farm. Ty rarely, if ever, played with black children. He did, however, claim that he learned to swim by holding onto the neck of a young African-American boy who would swim to the middle of a stream. He would then pull Ty from his neck, forcing him to swim to shore on his own. Ty also worked alongside African Americans in the fields.

Much like most children of the time, Ty fished and hunted. His family owned many dogs. He often took his favorite, Old Bob, exploring the countryside around his family farm. There, they would hunt raccoon, deer, and squirrel. As a hunter, he had the same excellent eye and quick reflexes that he would have as a baseball player.

Some of Ty's favorite childhood memories involve summer visits to his paternal grandfather, John "Squire" Cobb. His grandfather lived in the Smoky Mountains, near Murphy, North Carolina, about 110 miles (177 kilometers) from Royston. Today, 110 miles may not seem like a great distance, but this was before cars and highways. Making a trip of that distance was considered a major undertaking. Ty loved his grandfather very much. Along with his father, he was a man he could look up to and respect.

He especially loved taking long walks with his beloved "Granddaddy Johnny" in the Smoky Mountains. There, they would hunt, and his grandfather would entertain Ty with tales of Southern heroism during the Civil War. He would also tell Ty about his adventures hunting bears in the very woods they were exploring.

From early childhood, Ty showed some of the anger and antisocial tendencies he displayed as an adult. In his biography *Cobb*, Al Stump recounts the memories of two of Cobb's childhood friends. Bud Bryant recalled:

Oh, we had some fights, toe to toe stuff. He'd win one, next time I'd get the best of it. You couldn't make [him] stay down. Born to win. Touchy and stubborn about the smallest things. There were times he'd disappear or climb a tree and stay there for hours because his mother made him wash some kitchen pots or sing in church. Could never laugh it off when the joke was on him.

Another friend, Bob McCreary, remembered Ty's constant need to prove himself:

> He could throw a rock out of sight at 12 or so and outwrestle any of us at catch-as-catch-can not long later. He was always thinking of new things to try. Once, down at the pond, Ty said he could hold his breath underwater longer than any of us. We lasted maybe a minute, while he was still down there. Someone, probably Ty, invented the crazy trick of laying on a railroad track and being last to roll off before the locomotive got there. He didn't lose that one often.

The young Ty Cobb also showed signs of the competitive nature and quick temper that would stay with him through-out his life. As Richard Bak quotes Cobb in his biography, *Ty Cobb: His Tumultuous Life and Times*, "I was a boy with a vying nature. I saw no point in losing, if I could win." It was when he did not win that his temper would flare.

When Ty was 10 years old, he was suspended from the Royston District School for a few days. A spelling bee had taken place between boy and girl teams. When a male classmate missed a word and the girls' team won, Ty hit and kicked him. For additional punishment, William Cobb had his son clean out the farm's cowsheds.

As Al Stump reports in his book *Cobb*, Ty remembered the incident many years later. "I never could stand losing," he stated. "Second place didn't interest me. I had a fire in my belly."

This "fire in the belly" worried William Cobb. When Tyrus was visiting his grandfather during the summer, he would often receive letters from his father. They would urge him to learn to control his temper and to "stop your unsuit-able acts." These letters hurt Ty, who wanted nothing more than his father's approval.

After Ty received one such letter, his grandfather sug-gested he do something special to make his father happy. He thought that Ty might write an article about man's relation to the natural world. Ty could send it in to be published by the weekly Royston newspaper, now owned and edited by William Cobb.

Ty wrote an article called "Possums and Myself." According to Al Stump in his book *Cobb*, Ty praised "possums for their finer points," and then wrote about how he and Old Bob "treed 'Brother Possum' and how he'd shot, killed, gutted and skinned him, 'who felt no pain and made a fine cap for wearing.'"

William Cobb was pleased with the article, published it, and sent a copy to Ty along with the following letter: "You are making good progress in aligning yourself with the grand outdoors, yet always remember to remain in control of yourself, to be dutiful, to be proud, but courteously proud."

William Cobb may have been concerned about Ty's quick temper. In time, he would become even more concerned about his son's growing passion for baseball.

TY DISCOVERS BASEBALL

Professional baseball began in the United States around 1865. The National League was formed as the first true major league in 1876. Around this time, baseball was first referred to as "the national pastime."

It bears repeating that Ty Cobb grew up in a different era than today. There was no radio or television. There were no movies. Other sports, like football and basketball, were just being developed. But in nearly every American town, small and large, boys and men alike got together to play baseball. It was, as Richard Bak pointed out, "a national obsession."

Children were on their own in playing baseball. Public schools rarely offered sports as part of the curriculum. Organized Little League Baseball did not yet exist. (It would start up in 1939.) Young people had to organize games themselves.

Cobb's future teammate Sam Crawford had his own adventures on the road as a teenage ballplayer. As he recalled in Richard Bak's biography of Cobb:

Every town had its own town team in those days. One of the boys was a cornet player, and when we'd come to a town he'd whip out that cornet and sound off. People would all come out to see what was going on, and we'd announce that we were the Wahoo team and were ready for a ball game. Every little town out there on the prairie had its own ball team and ball grounds, and we challenged them all. We

☆ ☆ ☆ ☆ ☆

LITTLE LEAGUE

Little League did not exist when Ty Cobb was a boy. Since then, though, it has become an essential part of growing up for many children. Millions of children around the world have learned about baseball and teamwork by playing for their local Little League team.

The Little League was founded by Carl Stotz, a lumberyard clerk, in 1939. At its birth, it was a simple three-team league in Williamsport, Pennsylvania. Today, children in countries around the world—including Israel, Jordan, Russia, Mexico, Japan, China, and South Africa—all play the same game as children here in the United States.

The leagues have six divisions. These divisions are based on the ages of the children playing. The divisions are Tee Ball, Minors, Little (or Majors), Junior, Senior, and Big. Boys and girls from ages 5 to 18 are eligible to play. There is also a "Challenger Division" designed for children with disabilities.

Perhaps the most famous event in the Little League calendar is the annual Little League Baseball World Series. It is held in August of each year in South Williamsport, Pennsylvania. Tournaments leading up to the series are held throughout the United States and the world. In 2006, the Little League team from Columbus, Georgia, beat the Asian representative, from Kawaguchi City, Japan, to win the World Series.

didn't have any uniforms or anything, just baseball shoes maybe, but we had a manager. . .

Back in Royston, 12-year-old Ty discovered baseball. He was a batboy for the Royston Reds, a semiprofessional hometown team. Also, he played with the Royston Rompers, a town team of 12- to 16-year-olds.

His father disapproved of baseball and athletics. He felt that they were a waste of time. He saw them as a distraction from Ty's studies and chores on the farm. Because of his father's attitude, Ty knew that he would be unable to get money from his father to buy a bat and a glove.

At first, he made do with using a flat board as a bat, but that did not last long. He turned to making his own bats, whittled down from extra lumber normally used to make caskets. He named his favorite bat "Big Yellow." He even took it to bed with him.

His aunt Norah Chitwood encouraged him as a ballplayer. During his summers at his grandfather's, she would take him by buggy to play baseball in the small towns of Murphy and Andrews.

The boys whom Ty played with were bigger, stronger, and older than he was. Baseball as it was played then was a much rougher game than it is today. For example, base runners nowadays can be put out by being thrown out at the base or by being touched with the ball. Back then (although this practice was banned within just a few years), runners could also be put out by being hit with a thrown ball. In fact, defensive players were encouraged to throw the ball directly at the head of the base runner—all the better to knock him out for the rest of the game.

On one particularly memorable occasion, Ty hit a single and was running for second base when he was hit, or "soaked," as it was called, with a ball to his head. The next thing he knew,

Aunt Norah was taking him off the field. He was done playing for that day.

This rough style of play did contribute to his base-running style, which made him one of the greatest base runners and stealers the game has ever known. He learned to be an elusive target, to swerve unexpectedly, and to outthink everyone on the field.

He learned, as Al Stump relates in *Cobb*, by "watching the fielders' eyes, their jump on the ball, body lean, throwing and release habits—every little . . . thing about them . . . keeping one jump ahead of the defense."

Necessity also contributed to his distinctive batting style. Unlike most players, he held the bat with his hands wide apart on the handle. He developed this style because it was the only way that he could get around on the ball with his heavy home-made bats.

Ty also learned to stand as far back from the plate as he could. By doing so, he had just a bit more time, no more than a split second, to "read" the pitcher's intentions. This allowed him to respond better to the pitch. Although a split second may not seem like much, to a precision batter like Ty Cobb, it meant all the difference in the world.

His batting rapidly improved. One afternoon while playing in Murphy, he hit the ball 200 feet (61 meters) for a triple. Two runs scored, and his team won. Ty never forgot that game. For the first time, he felt like a real ballplayer, and he had won the respect of his team.

Back home in Royston, William Cobb was dead set against Ty playing baseball. One night, Ty came home from playing a game with the Rompers with his eye closed up after he was struck by a foul tip. As described in Stump's *Cobb*, his father was furious. "Stop it," he ordered his son. "There is nothing so useless on earth as knocking a string ball around a pasture with ruffians."

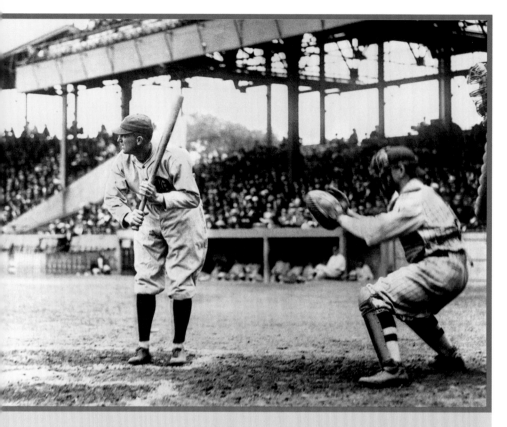

Ty Cobb's distinctive batting style—gripping the bat with his hands apart—developed when he was a teenager. He made his own bats, which were heavy. Holding the bat in this manner was the only way he could get around on the ball.

Ty's bats were taken away from him, and he was forbidden to play any more baseball. It took several months for Bob McCreary, a semipro player and a friend of William Cobb's, to persuade William to let Ty play baseball again. McCreary finally convinced him that baseball could help instill a badly needed sense of discipline in Ty. The game would also help him to build up his muscles. (Ty was still a fairly skinny kid.)

He promised William that he would keep an eye on Ty and keep him away from tobacco and liquor. (Baseball had such a bad reputation with the Professor, as William Cobb was known, that he assumed baseball would lead Ty directly to drinking and bad behavior.) William finally relented and allowed his son to return to the game.

Before too long, Ty began to stand out. In a game against Harmony Grove, Ty hit three singles and made a great catch at shortstop. The Professor, though, was determined that the time was near for Ty to focus on his education and to settle on a career. Baseball, in William Cobb's eyes, was a game played by boys, drunks, and men of bad character. He had higher aspirations for his son.

As a teacher, William Cobb had a strong belief in the importance of education. He knew that it was education that had made his own life possible. A well-educated, self-made man, he was far more than just a teacher and a farmer. He was, in fact, one of Royston's leading citizens.

He created, wrote for, and edited the local newspaper, the *Royston Record.* He had been elected mayor of Royston. He would go on to serve in the Georgia State Legislature. There, he worked hard to improve Georgia's public school system. In his spare time, he read classical literature and science. Is it any wonder that Ty looked up to his father with a sense of awe? Is it surprising that William Cobb had high expectations of his son?

William Cobb had hopes that his son would become a doctor. Ty had, in fact, at one time been apprenticed to a local doctor. He even assisted in the operation on a young African-American boy who had been shot in the stomach. With his sharp eyesight, he helped the doctor find where the bullet had lodged. Ty found the experience interesting, but he had no desire to study medicine.

If not medicine, William thought a career in the military might be just right for Ty. He felt that the structure, discipline, and regimentation that the military offered would help Ty learn to control his temper and "wild streak." With his political connections, William knew he would have little difficulty securing an appointment for his son at either the U.S. Military Academy at West Point, New York, or at the U.S. Naval Academy in Annapolis, Maryland. Again, though, Ty was just not interested.

For his part, Ty was unsure what he wanted to do when he grew up. What he knew for sure was that he *did not* want to be a farmer. Working in the fields in overalls embarrassed him. He would even hide rather than allow any girl he knew to catch him working hard, all hot and sweaty, on the farm.

Much to his father's dismay, school was not a high priority for Ty. Although intelligent, he never studied hard enough to do more than just pass any subject. All that really excited Ty was baseball.

It was hard, though, for him to imagine playing baseball professionally. For a small-town Southern boy, making the leap to the majors seemed nearly impossible. On the other hand, he knew baseball was the one thing that he was truly good at. Deep in his heart, he knew that he could excel at it.

As he later recalled, quoted in Richard Bak's *Cobb: His Tumultuous Life and Times*:

> It wasn't that I gave baseball a second thought as a career—skinny ninety pounder that I was. My overwhelming need was to prove myself a real man. In the classroom, I was merely adequate—except for a flair for oratory, which brought me a few prizes.
>
> I couldn't hope to match my celebrated father for brains. In town ball—pitted against older boys and men at the age of fourteen—was the chance to become more than another schoolboy and the son of Professor Cobb.

Ty would soon learn more about his true potential as a ballplayer. The first steps on his road to baseball immortality were about to begin.

What About Baseball?

In 1902, Ty Cobb was 15 years old. He was 5-foot-7 (170 centimeters) and skinny, weighing only 150 pounds (68 kilograms). He had a high-pitched voice, large ears, and pale skin.
He batted left-handed and threw with his right hand. And,
based on his reputation with the Rompers, he was given an
opportunity to try out for the Royston Reds, the semiprofessional hometown team.

Amazingly, he made the team. Of the 15 other roster
players, nine were in their twenties. The others were 30 years
old or older. Ty was by far the youngest, smallest, and least-
experienced player on the team. But as his old ally Bob
McCreary, who was now the manager of the Reds, remembered, he demonstrated enough talent to earn his spot on the
team. "Ty was a little, skinny, spare-built fellow," he recalled

in Richard Bak's *Cobb*, "but I thought at the time that he was about the best natural ballplayer I had ever seen."

William Cobb was not happy about his son's acceptance by the Reds. He decided, though, on a change of strategy. Rather than argue with his son, he decided to go along with Ty's desire to play baseball—for the time being. He thought and hoped that baseball would just be a passing fad and prayed that Ty would soon grow up and choose a "real" career.

Ty was too small for any of the Reds' uniforms. So his Aunt Norah again stepped in to help. She cut pieces of flannel, dyed them red, and made him his own uniform. He was ready to play.

In the beginning, his play was not terribly impressive. With his speed, he did well at baserunning. He also did his best at playing shortstop and outfield. Most of the time, though, he sat on the bench.

His father trusted McCreary so much that he allowed Ty to accompany the team for an away game. The game was played two counties away at Royston's rival, Elberton. Here, Ty had his first strong outing as a Red. Coming to bat as a left-hander, Ty noticed that Elberton accordingly moved its outfield to the right. At both of his at-bats, he adjusted his position at the plate and hit two strong singles to the left, down the third baseline. During the game, he also stole one base and initiated two double plays. The Reds won, 7-5. His teammates were so happy with his play that they even bought him a bacon sandwich to celebrate.

To young Ty, that game was a turning point. Many years later, as quoted in Al Stump's *Cobb,* he described his feelings to legendary sportswriter Grantland Rice: "That day the bat actually tingled in my hands. . . . It gave off an electrical impulse that shot through my body . . . a great feeling. . . . It told me I'd found something I could do extremely well."

In his own book *The Tumult and the Shouting: My Life in Sport,* Grantland Rice went on to say about Cobb, "From that start, Cobb never missed an opportunity to refine his craft. A man apart. The shrewdest athlete and perhaps the shrewdest man I've ever met."

TRIUMPH AND DISGRACE

One fielding play in a game against Harmony Grove briefly made Ty the talk of the town. It was the eighth inning. Ty was playing center field, and the bases were loaded, with two men out. The batter hit a high drive toward left field. Ty, seeing that the left fielder would not be able to make the play, dashed toward him. As the ball bounced off the left fielder's hand, Ty, moving behind him, caught the ball one-handed. In the process, he dove so hard for the ball that he crashed into a fence. Somehow, he managed to hold onto the ball, ensuring a victory for the Reds.

The play was so spectacular that even William Cobb had to acknowledge it. The *Royston Record*, which normally ignored sports stories, included a report of the game.

Ty's hot streak as a player continued. Diving, running, playing harder and faster than anyone else, he rapidly became a crowd favorite. Reds players were not paid. In those days, though, fans often threw change onto the field to their favorite players. After one game, Ty had earned $11—a huge sum of money back then.

He picked up extra cash in other ways as well. Other teams, not scheduled to square off against the Reds, wanted to see the young phenomenon play. The town of Anderson, South Carolina, offered him $2.50 per game to play against Harwell, Georgia. Ty accepted the offer but used an alias: "Jack Jones."

He was not worried about his father learning that he had accepted money to play. But, by taking the money, he had technically become a professional. Because of this, he would have been ineligible to play college sports if he chose to go to college. Hence, the deception.

But the $5 that Ty earned playing two games for Anderson did not last long. Ty needed to earn more money to buy a new fielder's glove. (A new style of glove had just appeared in

★ ★ ★ ★ ☆

BASEBALL GLOVES

Some people claim that, in 1870, Doug Allison, a catcher for the Cincinnati Red Stockings (now the Reds), was the first player to use a baseball glove. The first *documented* use of a glove, however, was by Charlie Waitt. Playing for St. Louis as a first baseman/outfielder in 1875, he wore a pair of flesh-colored gloves.

The early gloves were simply leather gloves with the fingers cut off. They would allow the same control as a bare hand, but with the benefit of added padding.

Still, the use of gloves caught on slowly. Many baseball players of the time thought it was "unmanly" to use a glove.

When baseball star Albert Spalding adopted the glove, more and more players began to use them. By the mid-1890s, most players used gloves in the field.

The basic design for the glove stayed the same until 1920. That was when Bill Doak, a pitcher for the St. Louis Cardinals, proposed a change. He thought that a web should be placed between the first finger and the thumb. This would create a pocket, making it even easier to catch the ball. His suggestion was quickly accepted. That design has become the standard for baseball gloves.

Interestingly, after his retirement, Albert Spalding and his brother opened a sporting-goods store in Chicago. The business quickly expanded into the manufacture of sporting goods—the Spalding line. Spalding is the leading manufacturer of baseball equipment, including balls, bats, and gloves. The company also went on to develop and manufacture the first American football, basketball, volleyball, and liquid-center golf ball.

Ty Cobb stretched to make a catch during practice with the Detroit Tigers. The widespread use of baseball gloves did not begin until the mid-1890s. The webbing between the thumb and the first finger did not come about until the 1920s.

stores.) He entered a turkey shoot, but did not win any prize. In desperation, he made what he felt was one of the biggest mistakes of his life.

As would be expected, his father owned a large personal library. Ty, thinking that a couple of books would never be missed, took two of them to sell.

Unfortunately, he tried to sell them to someone who knew his father and reported to him what Ty was trying to do. As Al Stump reports in *Cobb*, William Cobb was livid: "I thought I was raising a straight shooter, not a thief! Now you see why I consider baseball a bad business! Your associates are ruining you!"

Ty was devastated. Furious for making himself appear less in his father's eyes, he began to cry and beg for forgiveness. His punishment was harsh. He was not to play baseball for the Reds for an indeterminate period of time. Also, he was assigned plenty of extra farm duties. Forced to do the work he hated and not allowed to play the game he loved, the punishment was complete.

For Ty, the summer of 1902 was one of hard work and sweat. His father was away from home most of the summer, because of his work as a legislator. Ty worked harder than he ever had before. He hoped that, if he did a good job, his father would once again be proud of him. If that happened, he hoped, he would again be allowed to play baseball.

When William Cobb returned home in September, he was very pleased with the job that Ty had done. Besides his normal chores, Ty had been assigned a large plot of land for which he was wholly responsible. Equipment, purchasing, planting, bookkeeping—he was responsible for everything. William was happy to see that Ty had done as he had asked and displayed a new sense of responsibility. Ty had also learned a great deal about agriculture in the process.

William Cobb noted a physical change in Ty as well. A combination of hard work and a normal teenage growth spurt added 2 inches (5 centimeters) and 10 pounds (4.5 kilograms) of muscle to Ty's frame. He was becoming a man. And with that, the relationship between him and his father would never be the same.

His father began to listen to him. He started to take his son's opinions seriously. On a business trip to Athens, Georgia (one of the first sizable towns Ty had ever seen), he asked Ty serious questions about what livestock to buy. He even began to base his decisions on what Ty had to say. It was a proud moment for Ty.

As quoted in Stump's *Cobb,* he remembered, "It was the sweetest thing in the world to be finally accepted by my father. . . . All at once, he was willing to hear my ideas, to discuss them, and even exchange opinions. We'd talk about crop production. English export of cotton competed with our Georgia output, and I never felt closer to him than when he said, 'Do you think we should sell now, or hold on for a better price?'"

RETURN TO BASEBALL

In the spring of 1903, Ty was allowed to return to the Reds. The additional muscle he had put on only made him a better player. As Al Stump wrote in *Cobb,* "His added strength allowed Cobb, crouched low and far back in the box, to handle speed, curveball drops, and assorted other pitching with almost equal ability." He was batting so well that crowds as large as 600 people came out to watch him play. He estimated that his batting average was .450.

Now 16 years old, Ty had yet to see a big-league team play. He had heard that the Cleveland Blues (later to become the Indians) would be holding their spring training in Atlanta. He and a friend rode 100 miles (161 kilometers) in the back of a wheat wagon to watch them play an exhibition game.

Ty was entranced. One of his heroes, second baseman Napoleon Lajoie, was playing that day. He saw his idol get several

In 1903, 16-year-old Ty Cobb and a friend traveled to Atlanta in the back of a wagon to see Napoleon Lajoie *(above)* play in an exhibition game. Seven years later, Cobb and Lajoie would spend the season battling it out for the American League batting championship.

base hits. Also while in Atlanta, Ty bought two books on baseball: *Scientific Baseball* by Fred Pfeffer and *A Ballplayer's Career* by Adrian "Cap" Anson, a legendary player in the late 1800s.

Ty read and reread the books, underlining what he thought was important and filling the margins with notes. Ty was continuously studying and thinking about baseball technique and strategy. He was always looking for ideas on how to improve his game, to help give him an edge over other players.

He knew, though, that his chances of making it to the major leagues were next to impossible. About the highest level that Cobb, playing in the South, could realistically hope to reach was the Southern League, a Class-A league. Very, very few players were able to make the leap from there to the majors.

In the fall of 1903, Ty learned about a new Class-C circuit. It was called the South Atlantic, or "Sally," League. Ty was determined to try out for one of the teams. Ty sent letters of application to all six teams in the new league. His letter, as he later recalled to Al Stump in *Cobb*, read something like this:

> Sir:
>   I play the infield and outfield for a good team here. I lead the Royston team first in batting, second in fielding. Knowing you have many fine players, I feel I could do much better with your coaching. Please consider my application to try out with (name of club) for the 1904 season.
>   Yrs. truly,
>   Tyrus Cobb

Ty did not tell his father about his plans.

Days and weeks went by without a response. Ty began to fear that nobody would answer his application. Then, he finally received one letter, from Cornelius Strouthers, the manager and part-owner of the Augusta Tourists. It read:

> Tyrus Cobb:
>   This will notify you that you are free to join our spring training practice with the understanding that you pay your own expenses. Reply promptly.

Ty immediately answered back and soon received a contract in the mail. It promised him $50 a month (the average pay for a rookie in the Sally League) *if* he made the team. He would also have to bring his own uniform. He would be issued an official Tourists uniform if he made the team.

"If that one team hadn't answered," Cobb wrote in his autobiography, "I wonder if I'd even have made baseball a career, for my ambition hung by a tenuous thread . . . suspended between my duty to my father, and my own desire."

He began by informing his mother of his decision. A quiet, reserved woman, she gave Ty her reluctant approval. She told Ty, though, that the final decision would be up to his father. She would not get involved.

Afraid of what might happen, Ty waited until the night before he was to leave for Augusta before telling his father. To Ty's considerable surprise, William Cobb did not shout and yell at his son. He barely even raised his voice. Instead, he quietly and methodically tried to persuade his son that he was making a big mistake. Instead of using his muscles, he tried to explain, Ty should be using his brains.

In Stump's *Cobb*, Ty vividly recalled the entire conversation: "This is a fool's act. I ask you to reconsider. You are only seventeen and at a crucial path. One path leads to a rewarding future, the other will leave you shiftless, a mere muscle-worker. I ask you again, reconsider."

The discussion continued until three in the morning, but Ty was not to be dissuaded. "I signed that contract because I want to find out what I can do," he told his father. "I'm almost sure I can make good. I'll stay out of trouble."

William Cobb was forced to give in and allow his son to follow his dream. "Well, son, you have chosen. So be it. Go get it out of your system, and let us hear from you once in a while," he told his son. Obviously, William still held hope that baseball would just be a passing fancy. Once Ty got it out of his system, he could go to college and move into a "respectable" career.

Once he gave Ty his permission, William did what he could to help him out. He wrote out six checks for $15 each to cover Ty's expenses until he got paid. He also gave him $20 in cash for traveling money.

And he gave him some last words of advice. "I don't want to hear you've been drinking or around bad women." Ty promised to behave himself.

So at the age of 17, Ty left home, hopeful to begin a career in baseball. He knew that he was still a young man and not fully grown. He knew that he would be playing against mature, more experienced adults. He knew that he still had a lot to learn about baseball.

He also knew that this opportunity with the Tourists might be his big break. He was determined to do his very best and not let himself or his father down.

Early Struggles

The next day, Ty Cobb rode the train 80 miles (129 kilometers) to Augusta, Georgia. There, he checked into a cheap hotel. Heading out to Warren Park, he learned that 35 players were trying out for only 16 spots on the team. He would have his work cut out for him.

Players already on the team made no effort to help or be nice to the boys trying to earn a spot. New players, after all, could become a threat to their jobs. The older players kept the new ones from taking batting practice. Ty spent a good deal of time in the field, running down and catching foul balls hit off the bats of the older players. The rest of the time he spent on the bench.

He was eager to please. He could not understand that the hazing he and the others were receiving was a standard practice

When Ty Cobb was trying out for the Augusta Tourists in the spring of 1904, the Detroit Tigers played the Tourists in an exhibition game. After the game, Cobb asked Tiger right fielder Sam Crawford *(above)* for fielding tips, and Crawford helped the teenager out for an hour. Just a few years later, Crawford and Cobb would be teammates, but not friends.

at that time. New players often found their uniforms ripped to shreds or their shoes nailed to the floor. Ty's experiences were no different. Cornelius Strouthers, the manager, did nothing to help Cobb or any of the other young hopefuls. "You make your own place here," he said as quoted in Stump's *Cobb*.

Ty did get the opportunity to watch the Detroit Tigers play the Tourists in an exhibition game. Sitting on the bench, he had the chance to study Detroit's left-handed right fielder, Wahoo Sam Crawford.

At one of Crawford's turns at bat, Ty watched him go to first base after being walked. Crawford noted that the Tourists were off guard, and he suddenly took off running, making it safely to second base for a steal. Cobb filed this move away, hoping to be able to use it himself one day.

After the game, he went to Crawford and asked him for fielding tips. Crawford was impressed at Cobb's eagerness to improve, and for the next hour, he shared what he had learned over the years. Cobb would always be grateful to Crawford for his generosity. Years later, Cobb played alongside Crawford on the Tigers. At that time, their relationship would definitely change.

On opening day of the Tourists' regular season, Ty was surprised to learn that he would be playing. The Tourists' regular first baseman, Harry Bussey, was holding out for more money. So, the regular center fielder, Mike McMillan, was moved to first, and Ty took his place in center field, batting seventh.

Using his unusual grip (his left hand holding the bat six to seven inches above his right), Cobb got to bat three times that first game. His first at-bat, he grounded out. His next at-bat, he hit an inside-the-park home run. His last at-bat, he hit a double right up the middle. Not bad for his first game.

Even the local newspaper took notice. In its report on the game, the *Augusta Chronicle* noted, "Outfielder T. Cobb was auspicious in his first local showing. . . . Four-base and two-base pry-ups are a better act than one could expect from a beginner."

In his first game, the crowd had cheered and the newspaper had praised him. Perhaps because of this, his manager and teammates continued to show indifference, if not dislike, to their youngest player. In his second game with the Tourists, it is unclear if he actually got a hit, but he did get his first stolen base. It would not, however, make any difference to the Tourists' management.

After the game, he was summoned to Strouthers's office. There, he was told that he would not be receiving a contract. An agreement had been reached with Bussey, the first baseman. McMillan was being moved back to center field. Despite his performance in his first two games, there was no room on the roster for Ty Cobb.

Ty was crushed. He had left Royston with such high hopes—and now this. He had no job and no prospect for future employment. He had already spent part of the money his father had given him. Going home to Royston as a failure was unthinkable. He could not bear the thought of calling his father and letting him know that he had failed. What was he going to do?

Furious at Strouthers and the Tourists for not giving him a chance, he briefly considered giving up on baseball. He had written to the other five teams in the Sally League but had received no response. He had even applied for a position as a clerk in a cotton warehouse, but no jobs were available. Maybe, he thought, he would have to give up. He could go to the University of Georgia, as his father wanted, and study medicine. For a time, that move seemed to be the best solution to his problem.

One day, though, he fell into a conversation with a young pitcher who had also been cut from the Tourists. His name was Thad "Mobile Kid" Hayes. Hayes had an idea. The city of Anniston, Alabama, had a semipro team that played three to five games a week.

The Anniston Steelers were part of a semipro league, not a nationally recognized minor league. Some of the players, though, were so good that scouts for Class-A teams came out to watch them play. Hayes had heard that Anniston needed a pitcher and an outfielder. He had also heard that the team paid $50 to $60 a month. Maybe, Hayes thought, they should give it a try.

Before he could go, Ty knew that he would need to call his father. After letting him know what had happened in Augusta, his father asked him what he would do next. Ty explained to his father about the possibility of playing for Anniston. What his father said next, as quoted in Al Stump's *Cobb*, surprised him:

> "If you get hired there, you'll be leaving the state. Getting farther from home. However, I don't like the idea of you giving up. To quit is the easy way out. Is playing ball still important to you?"
>
> "Yes, it is," said Ty.
>
> "Then go on to this Alabama place. Stay away from drink. Do your best to succeed. You have my blessing. I don't like quitters. . . . *Don't come home a failure!*"

Ty was shocked. His father was actually encouraging him to continue to play baseball. His decision was made. He would go to Anniston.

ANNISTON STEELERS

Ty Cobb and Thad Hayes reported to the Steelers on May 2, 1904. Playing conditions with the unsanctioned team were rough. The team used one baseball per game, no matter how much of a beating it took. Players shared only one bathtub. They traveled from game to game in a horse and buggy. Often, lunch was nothing but a bowl of bean soup. Dinner, a plate of hog jowls and grits.

For this, he received $50 a month. He had to pay for his own lodgings. He still could not afford to purchase a decent glove. Ty calculated that by the end of the season, he would be completely out of money. None of that mattered, though. He was playing baseball.

Ty soon discovered that he could play the game as well as anyone else in the league. He could run faster, he had a great arm, and he could hit to all sides of the field. He had learned that, by opening up his stance at the last moment, he could hit the ball pretty much wherever he wanted.

He also began to learn to bunt. Ty not only bunted as a sacrifice but to get a hit for himself. Many of these skills he learned through the tips he had picked up from Wahoo Sam Crawford.

Ty was soon among the league's top hitters with a .350 batting average. He also picked up a number of fans, including a local steel-mill executive named J.B. Darden. Darden invited the Steelers' new sensation to live in his home and offered him free room and board. He even talked the Steelers' management into raising Ty's salary to $65 a month.

He certainly earned his money. In one game against Oxford, Alabama, he hit for the cycle—one single, one double, one triple, and one home run all in one game. According to Al Stump, he would have gotten credit for a second home run as well but was cheated out of it.

The left fielder had pretended to catch Cobb's ball as it went over the fence. What he actually did was substitute a ball he had hidden in his pocket for the ball Cobb had hit. Ty knew exactly what had happened and attacked the left fielder.

A brawl started. The benches on both sides cleared, and even some members of the crowd got involved in the fighting. When the melee finally settled down, the umpire threw Cobb out of the game.

Cobb went ballistic. (Years later, he claimed that it was just an act, but nobody at the time thought he was kidding.) He swore, shoved, and spat at the umpire. With that, the whole

Grantland Rice, pictured here in a photo from the 1940s, was a popular sportswriter in Georgia in the early 1900s. Ty Cobb secretly sent
to Rice and other writers postcards praising the talents of a youngster
named Cobb who was playing for the Anniston Steelers. Rice then wrote
about Cobb in one of his columns.

riot began again. Play was delayed for nearly an hour before the
dust-up settled down for the second time. Ty was forced to give
up one day's pay as a fine.

The ejection was Ty's first from a game, but it would not be his last. Ty's reaction? As he told Al Stump, "One of the best fights I was ever in. People got to know me."

The fight helped to get Ty the attention as a ballplayer that he craved. How could he get more? He was playing for a team in a new, unsanctioned, and unnoticed league. How was he going to get the attention of the teams in Class-A leagues, let alone the majors? He would have to take matters into his own hands.

MASTER OF PUBLICITY

At the time, Grantland Rice was one of the most popular sportswriters in the state of Georgia. He wrote for the *Atlanta Journal*. (He would soon go on to become the most famous sportswriter in all of the United States.) Rice began to receive telegrams, letters, and postcards, all of them praising the talents of the Anniston Steelers' young player, Tyrus Cobb.

"Tyrus Raymond Cobb, the dashing young star with Anniston, Ala., is going great guns. He is as fast as a deer and undoubtedly a phenom," said one, as cited in Bak's *Cobb*. Others made comments like, "Keep your eye on Cobb . . . he's one of the finest players I've ever seen," and "Have you seen Ty Cobb play ball yet? He is the fastest mover in the game."

Faced with a barrage of mail praising a player he had yet to see, Rice finally wrote about Cobb in his column. He said, as quoted in Richard Bak's biography of Cobb, "Rumors had reached Atlanta from numerous sources that over in Alabama there's a young fellow named Cobb who seems to be showing an unusual lot of talent." Other sportswriters who had also received the same letters wrote similar columns.

Not until many years later did Cobb confess to Grantland Rice, by then his friend, that he had been the author of all of those letters. When Rice asked Cobb why he had resorted to such trickery, Cobb responded simply, "I was in a hurry."

The plan worked. Rice's article came to the attention of the Augusta Tourists, now playing under a new manager,

Andy Roth. (Cobb had vowed never to play for their old manager, Cornelius Strouthers, again.) The Tourists were having a poor season and decided to give Ty a second chance.

☆ ☆ ☆ ☆ ☆

STEALING BASES

Timing is critical to stealing a base. The runner who is trying to steal must start to run as soon as the pitcher has committed to throwing the pitch to home plate. If the runner starts too soon, the pitcher may throw to a base instead of home plate to pick off the runner. If the runner starts too late, the catcher is likely to be able to throw to the base he is heading to and get him out.

The base most often stolen is second base. It is the farthest from home plate, so the catcher has a longer throw to prevent the steal. Third base is a shorter throw. An attempt to steal third becomes easier, however, with a right-handed batter at the plate, because the catcher has to throw around the batter.

Stealing home requires aggressiveness because the ball will almost certainly arrive at the plate before the runner. Ty Cobb has the most steals of home plate in a season (8) and a career (54) in Major League Baseball history. In the last few decades, players have rarely tried to steal home. If such a steal is attempted, it is usually done as a delayed double steal—the runner at first base tries to steal second, while the runner at third base heads for home once the catcher makes the throw to second base.

In Cobb's day, base stealing was popular in the major leagues. Its use fell off when Babe Ruth and power hitting came into vogue. Stealing bases regained prominence in the 1960s with Maury Wills of the Los Angeles Dodgers, who broke Cobb's single-season record for stolen bases in 1962. That mark was later broken by Lou Brock in 1974 and Rickey Henderson in 1982.

Having spent less than 100 days in Anniston, he was recalled back to Augusta.

Initially, he did not play his best. It is important to remember that he still was only 17 years old. He had not reached his full physical development. He was playing against experienced adults. Ty was probably the youngest player in the league, if not in all of professional baseball. He had been able to keep up with the players in Anniston. His size and inexperience, however, showed in his playing for Augusta.

He had disagreements with Roth over base running. Roth played what was even then considered "old school" baseball. He wanted Cobb to steal bases rarely and then only under the direction of the base coach. Cobb was convinced that he knew best. He was playing a newer style of baseball. He trusted his own intuition, eyesight, and sense of timing to know when to steal.

As Al Stump described it, "Whether he was aware of it or not, he was constructing a foundation for detecting openings and instantly exploiting them, confusing infields. Even if he was thrown out by a yard on a base-advance attempt, he had established the threat that he might go at any moment, especially when the odds were against him."

Roth hated what he saw as Cobb's stunts and theatrics. The crowds, however, loved them. After one game in Charleston, South Carolina, when Cobb was thrown out twice while stealing bases after ignoring Roth's signs, he was fined and kept on the bench for two days.

Ty ended the season batting only .237 in just 37 games. More than half of his hits had been singles. He had been caught stealing in almost half of his attempts. Ty returned home to Royston to consider his future.

Although confident in his abilities, he had doubts as to whether the Tourists would call him back for another season. Given his lackluster performance as well as his difficulties with Roth, not returning was definitely a possibility.

While in Royston, Cobb again considered the possibility of giving up on baseball for either medicine or the military. In addition, he was dating, or "courting" a girl, as it was called then. She came from one of Royston's leading families. It was doubtful that her parents would ever approve of her marrying a baseball player. For Ty, this was one more reason to consider going back to school and pursuing a "respectable" career.

Ty kept busy that winter working on his father's farm. He also took a job working in the cotton sheds of a company in Carnesville, Georgia. That job gave him much of the knowledge that allowed him to invest wisely in cotton while playing for the Detroit Tigers. His smart investments helped make him one of the wealthiest athletes of his day.

Although he claimed to still be considering college, it was obvious to all who knew him that he planned to stay with baseball. He worked hard to stay in shape. He was seen daily doing a combination of jogging and fast sprints for five to six miles, no matter what the weather.

It was apparent that Ty did not seriously intend to give up baseball. His girlfriend's father banned Ty from his house. He would not allow Ty to date his daughter ever again. To him, an aspiring baseball player was not the sort of man for his daughter.

Much to Ty's relief, in the spring of 1905, he received a letter from Andy Roth. In it, he asked Ty to return to Augusta for the upcoming season. Ty responded that he would be delighted to return. He added, though, that he would need more money—$125 a month.

The request was quite a gamble on Ty's part. Why should Roth nearly double his salary? Cobb argued that if he did not get the raise, he might just sit out the season. He even might, he said, quit baseball entirely and go to college.

Ty made the same threats to Bill Croke, the president of the Tourists. Croke, who saw Cobb's speed, batting ability, and potential for growth (as well as his growing popularity among fans), gave in. Ty got his $125 a month. Ty was learning how to negotiate, stand his ground, and get his way with management.

He started the season playing left field. He preferred center field, which gave him more opportunities to make plays. He was also unhappy with his hitting. He started off the season slowly, batting under .260. However, by June, he had raised his average to .320, ranking him second best among the Tourists.

He also began to improve as a base runner. He had always been extraordinarily fast. Now he began to play mind games with the fielders. For example, when standing at first base, he would pretend he had been injured. He would call for a doctor and be sure to be seen "walking it off." Then, just when the fielders were convinced that he would be unable to run, let alone steal, he would dash off to second.

He would do anything to gain an advantage. His goal was to use psychology to get a fielder to make a mistake on a throw or a catch. He knew if he could do that, he would have an opportunity to advance, or even to score.

Ty continued to clash with Roth. He so infuriated Roth with his attention-getting antics (eating a big bag of popcorn while playing left field, for example) that one day Roth announced that he had sold Cobb's contract to Charlotte. The price? $25—the cost of a mule. Cobb was furious and ready to go home. He was on the verge of quitting baseball forever.

The Tourists' president went to Cobb to calm him down. Andy Roth was in the process of being replaced as manager, so he no longer had the authority to make any decisions regarding trades. Cobb agreed to stay. His new manager, George Leidy, would turn out to be just the man to help Ty get to the next level.

Triumph
and Tragedy

Ty Cobb was fortunate to have George Leidy make the move from the Tourists' outfield to the position of manager. Without him, it is possible that Cobb would not have had another friend or ally on the team.

Many of the players on the Tourists resented and disliked Cobb. Some of this disdain was because of his obvious talent as a baseball player. Cobb responded to the team's dislike by withdrawing into himself. He became a loner. He would not socialize with the other players after games or on days off. Instead, he went on long walks and went fishing. While fishing, he often read, usually biographies of military heroes like Stonewall Jackson and Napoleon Bonaparte.

With his attitude and hot temper, he even managed to drive away the few players who had remained his friends. One such person was George Napoleon Rucker, who had been his room-mate for a time.

Since facilities at the Tourists' ballpark were limited, Cobb generally tried to beat his roommate back to their shared room so that he could be first to take a hot bath after a game. On one occasion, though, Rucker beat Cobb back to the room and was comfortably soaking in the tub when Cobb entered the room.

Cobb was furious, by Rucker's account, as quoted in Al Stump's *Cobb*. He grabbed Rucker and tried to drag him out of the bathtub. Unable to do so, he pulled his fist back to punch Rucker. "'You gone crazy?' yelled Rucker. Cobb stared at him—'with the wildest eyes I've ever seen in a human,' claimed Rucker later. . . . 'You don't understand!' Cobb gritted. *'I've got to be first at everything—all the time!'* "

This moment is an interesting and revealing one. It demonstrated Cobb's drive always to be the best, to be first. That trait is admirable and necessary for an athlete. When applied to life off the field, however, it easily turns into a destructive force. After the incident, Rucker found himself a new roommate, and Cobb stayed at a different boarding house than his teammates did.

Around this time, George Leidy reached out to Cobb. Playing next to him in the outfield, he had gained an appreciation for Cobb's strengths and weaknesses as an athlete. He also knew that Cobb had reached a plateau as a player. He was stuck, unable to improve his game to the next level. He was also frustrated by his relations with his teammates and with management. He was losing his sense of excitement about playing baseball. Leidy decided that it was time to take Cobb under his wing and have a talk with him.

Leidy would take Cobb out walking, and they would stop and sit on a park bench. Leidy would do most of the talking. He told Cobb about how baseball was growing. He described the new stadiums that were being built for major-league baseball teams in big cities across the country. He explained that baseball was rapidly becoming big business and that players' salaries were increasing at a fast pace. He carefully pointed out that nobody ever made the majors without years of hard work. As he had demonstrated, the rewards for all that work could be enormous.

Finally, he came to the heart of the matter, as Cobb related in his autobiography:

> You don't know what you've got. It's my belief that in a year or two, no more, you can be up there making ten times what you're getting now. For one thing, you have faster reactions and more breakaway speed than almost anyone I've seen, and I've seen the best of them. I'm sure you can become a better hitter than ninety-nine percent of the big boys. But it won't happen if you don't straighten up. Stop breaking training. Stay sober. Apply yourself every minute. You're not playing ball, you're playing at it.

For Cobb, this talk was a turning point in his career. For the first time since Bob McCreary had done so back in Royston, someone had tried to encourage him as a player. According to Cobb's autobiography, Leidy ended by putting his hand on Cobb's shoulder, promising him, "You can go down in the history books, have every lad in America idolizing you." With that, Cobb decided to take baseball and his career much more seriously.

Before this talk, he had gotten by on his natural talent and drive. Now, he would put in the extra effort it took to become great.

He began to practice virtually nonstop. Leidy threw him all kinds of pitches, teaching Cobb to hit anything that could be thrown at him. He taught Cobb to choke up farther on the bat, which gave him greater control. He fixed Cobb's stride and his stance. He taught him how to take a moment to watch

A young Ty Cobb batted during a game in the early 1900s. In 1905, when Ty was again playing for the minor-league Augusta Tourists, manager George Leidy gave Ty encouragement to reach the majors. The two worked together on his game, including his hitting, and Ty improved greatly.

the pitch, to see the spin and determine where the ball would be traveling.

He showed how Cobb's front shoulder, pointing at the pitcher, should remain there as long as possible. That split-second delay would allow Cobb to hit late-breaking curves as well as outside pitches. He worked with Cobb on his follow-through, on the hit-and-run, the drag bunt, and the double steal.

He learned how to draw out the third baseman by pretending to bunt, then hit the ball clean past him. Leidy taught Cobb the importance of snapping the wrists as an additional source of power. It was a master class in the art of hitting, and Cobb's batting quickly improved.

Leidy taught Cobb more than just hitting. For years, Cobb had slid into base head first. Leidy taught him to slide in feet first, which was much safer for the runner. It minimized head and neck injuries. It also cut down on the chances of getting his face stomped on by a fielder.

Ty quickly learned all of the variations of the feet-first slide. He also learned to use his spikes as a weapon. He learned to drive them into the legs and arms of any fielder who dared get in his way on the base path. Sometimes, he practiced sliding so much that the skin was completely rubbed off of his hips.

His game greatly improved. Ty Cobb was beginning to get noticed. Rumors spread that scouts from the majors were being sent out to check on the newly inspired player.

To Cobb's dismay, his father had still never seen him play.

It appeared, though, that he had come to accept having a baseball player as a son. Baseball was gaining in respectability, and Ty's growing reputation did nothing to embarrass William Cobb, as he had previously feared. Indeed, it was said that he carried in his wallet at all times a quotation from Grantland Rice praising Ty.

Still, Ty was disappointed that his father, the man he respected and loved more than anyone in the world, had not come to a game. In his notebook, as cited in Stump's biography *Cobb*, Ty, still only 18 years old, wrote, "I hope Father comes out to see me play someday." Unfortunately, that would never happen.

"THE BLACKEST OF DAYS"

As discussed in Stump's biography of Cobb, at 10 A.M. on August 9, 1905, Cobb received the following telegram. It was

★ ★ ★ ★ ☆

THE SCOUT

When Heinie Youngman, a scout with the Detroit Tigers, first met Ty Cobb, the young player did not make a good first impression—at least not until he got on the field. The Tigers had been hearing about George Leidy's work with Ty and sent Youngman to Augusta to take a look.

To Youngman, Ty was the picture of an ideal ballplayer, physically. Youngman told Ty he would like to ask him some personal questions. Ty said he could if he did not mind that Ty might not answer them.

"That was strike one against him," Youngman told Detroit's manager, according to Al Stump's *Cobb*. "Here I was giving a kid down in the sticks a chance to be noticed, and he's telling me that maybe, or maybe not, he'll talk." Ty gave brief answers, saying he did not drink whiskey, would be 19 in December, was unmarried, and had a high school education. He bragged a bit about his father, but when asked about his mother, he only said, "She cooks."

Youngman gave up on the questions and just decided to watch. Ty had two clutch hits and made a diving catch, and that was enough for Youngman. He told the Tigers that maybe, in a pinch, Ty could help the team.

from Joe Cunningham, a boyhood friend in Royston. (In telegrams, the word "STOP" takes the place of a period at the end of a sentence.)

COME AT ONCE STOP VERY SORRY STOP
YOUR FATHER DEAD IN SHOOTING
ACCIDENT STOP HURRY

Cobb made a frantic phone call to Royston but was unable to find out any details. Arriving home, he quickly learned what had happened. It was nearly impossible for him to believe. William Cobb had indeed been shot and killed, and it was Ty's mother, Amanda, who had pulled the trigger.

What exactly happened on the night of August 8 has been shrouded in rumor and mystery. The only known witness to the shooting was Amanda Cobb herself. Some facts, though, are fairly clear.

Amanda Cobb was at the family's house in town. William Cobb left the house that evening, saying that he was going out to the farm and would not be home for a couple of days. The younger children were staying at the house of friends. That night, when darkness fell, Amanda locked the doors of the house and went to bed.

What Amanda did not know was that William had not gone to the farm. Instead, around midnight, he climbed up a ladder to the second-floor landing outside their bedroom. He had a loaded pistol in his pocket. Amanda, hearing someone outside the bedroom window, saw what she described as a shadowy figure opening a window. She reached for the fully loaded, double-barreled shotgun that was always kept by the bed. She shot once, waited a moment, and then shot again. The first shot tore through William Cobb's stomach. The second shot blew off the top of his skull.

Immediate questions arose. Why did William Cobb come back home? Why did he try to enter the house through

An adult Ty Cobb is pictured in an undated photograph with his mother, Amanda Cobb. On August 8, 1905, Amanda Cobb fatally shot her husband and Ty's father, William Cobb. The full story behind the shooting has never been known. Two weeks later, Ty Cobb was called up by the Detroit Tigers to play in the major leagues. His father had never seen him play baseball.

a second-floor bedroom window? Why did he have a loaded pistol with him? Why were the windows closed on a hot, humid Georgia night?

Rumors quickly spread through the small town. It was said that Amanda Cobb was seeing another man when her husband was away on his many trips out of town. According to the rumors, William Cobb had heard these stories. He had come back to town and was climbing through the window in an attempt to catch Amanda red-handed with her boyfriend. It was then that the tragedy took place.

On August 10, two days after the shooting, a coroner's jury charged Amanda Cobb with voluntary manslaughter. Ty stood by his mother in the courtroom. The jury also announced that she would not be formally arrested until after the funeral.

On August 11, William Cobb's funeral was held. The next day, the county sheriff arrested Amanda Cobb. She posted bail of $7,000 and went home to await her trial.

Ty, understandably, was distraught. His mother was going on trial for voluntary manslaughter, and his father, his beloved father—he would never get to see again. William Cobb would never be able to see his son play baseball. Ty Cobb would never be able to show his father that he had made the right decision in becoming a ballplayer.

He told his best friend, Joe Cunningham, as quoted in Stump's *Cobb:* "I'll never get over this." Cunningham believed that this was true. He said:

> I know for a fact that he never got over it. It was like he took an oath in W.H.'s name. . . . A lot of what he'd done until then in playing ball was to win his father's respect . . . his admiration. . . . It was always on his mind that his father would never see him in action, crowds cheering him, all that. . . . The thing is W.H. opposed his playing ball. But he cared enough to let Ty go and prove he was a man. Ty owed him for that, and he never stopped paying back.

On August 15, Ty visited his father's grave and then returned to Augusta. In his first game back, Ty hit a single and a double and stole a base. Despite his enormous loss, he was able to still go out and play the game well, as he knew his father would have wanted him to do.

On August 19, just 11 days after his father's death, Ty got the news that seemed an impossible dream. He was being called up to the major leagues. The Detroit Tigers wanted him to join the team. Imagine his excitement. Imagine his sadness in knowing that he would never be able to tell his father the good news. Remember that he was only 18 years old.

6

The Big Leagues

Ty Cobb's final game with the Augusta Tourists was on August 25, 1905. The game was temporarily stopped when Cobb's fans presented him with a bouquet of flowers and a gold watch. The next day, he got on a train for the trip to Detroit.

It was a good time to be going up to the majors. Attendance at major-league games had jumped from 3.6 million in 1900 to 5.8 million in 1905. Also, the National League had been joined by a new league, the American League, in 1901. The first "World's Series" between the two leagues took place in 1903. The series was won by the new kids on the block, the American League's Boston Americans (soon to be the Red Sox).

Not only was baseball prospering, but so was the city of Detroit. The automobile industry was in its infancy. Companies like Ford, Buick, and Packard were opening factories. With these factories came a huge growth in population as people flocked to Detroit in search of jobs. Detroit soon became one of the country's largest and most prosperous cities. In 1905, Detroit was the country's thirteenth-largest city—by far the biggest city that Cobb had ever seen. It was his first "Yankee" city as well.

That he had been called up at all was a mixture of economics and luck. In April 1905, the Tigers owed the Tourists $500 for spring-training expenses. Short on cash, the Tigers left behind pitcher Eddie Cicotte to cover the debt. In return, Augusta gave Detroit the right to select any player at a later date for an equal amount.

By the end of August, with only one month left in the regular season, the Tigers needed a replacement player because of injuries in their outfield. Tiger scout Heinie Youngman had previously noticed Cobb. Also, Cobb came cheap. That was why he was selected. To the Tigers, he was just an end-of-season replacement. Nobody expected great things from him. And nobody expected that he would be asked to stick around once the season was over.

Cobb arrived in Detroit on August 29. He knew no one in the city, and no one was at the station to meet him. Again, remember that he was just 18 years old. He was in a big city for the first time in his life. He found a cheap hotel near the ballpark. The next day, he took a horse-cab to Bennett Park and introduced himself to his new manager, Bill Armour.

Much to Cobb's surprise, Armour had scheduled him to play that very day. He would be playing center field and batting fifth against the New York Highlanders (later renamed the Yankees).

Cobb came up to bat for the first time in the majors, against Jack Chesbro, an ace pitcher whose specialty was the spitball. The previous season, Chesbro had won an amazing 41 games, which is still a record.

As was his habit, Cobb came up to the plate swinging three bats to warm up. He had discovered that, by doing this, the single bat felt much lighter and faster after he dropped the extra two bats. Detroit fans had never seen anything like it.

Cobb swung and missed the first pitch, then took a called strike on the second pitch. His third pitch in the majors, he hit into the gap in left-center field for a run-scoring double. Cobb went hitless the rest of the game and was thrown out trying to steal second after being walked. He had definitely been noticed, though. The *Detroit Free Press* wrote, "Cobb, the rookie, may consider a double and a walk a much better career opener than usually comes a young ballplayer's way."

His good fortune continued the following day when he had two singles against the Highlanders. Although Cobb played in every one of the Tigers' final 41 games, he ended the season with a batting average of only .240. His play was erratic. It was sometimes great, but just as often it was sloppy and mistake-ridden. Cobb was still just a kid. He was playing against a whole new level of player. And it showed.

Cobb was uncertain if he would be offered a contract for the 1906 season. With no word from the Tigers as late as December, Cobb was on the verge once again of giving up baseball. Perhaps, he thought, he could coach college ball.

In January, he received the contract he had been hoping for. It was a full contract for the 1906 season, raising his salary to $1,500 a year. Obviously, he had shown enough talent to impress the Tigers' management. The contract and raise demonstrated the Tigers' confidence in their new player's potential.

Still, his position on the team was tenuous at best. He would be a backup player to the regular outfielders—Matty McIntyre in left field, Davy Jones in center field, and his old advisor, Wahoo Sam Crawford in right. Cobb was the low man on the totem pole. He knew that he could be traded or sold to another team at any time.

Wielding three bats, Ty Cobb waited in the on-deck circle for his turn at the plate. Before his first at-bat as a Tiger, Cobb warmed up swinging three bats. The fans in Detroit had never seen anything like it. Cobb practiced in this way because the single bat felt much lighter after he dropped the other two bats.

Despite this, Cobb should have felt good about himself. He had, against all odds, made it to the major leagues. He was, however, about to enter the period that he referred to, in Bak's *Cobb*, as "the most miserable and humiliating experience I've ever been through."

As spring training began in 1906, so did his teammates' harassment, their continuous hazing of Cobb. As the *Sporting News* described it, "His teammates wanted no part of someone who might one day take somebody's job. They banded to run him off the club with some of the hardest hazing ever seen."

Cobb had experienced hazing before, but never like this. Players blocked the way to the cage for batting practice. They turned away when he tried to speak with them. They tied his clothes in knots. His shoes were nailed to the floor. He was kept out of the bathroom until all the hot water had been used. Food was thrown at him in the dining room. His glove was ripped. Two of his favorite homemade bats were broken.

As Al Stump described it, someone even left a note on Cobb's hotel room door, saying, "LEAVE HERE WHILE YOU STILL CAN." After receiving the note, Cobb went out and bought a gun. He always carried it with him.

Why did Cobb receive such harsh treatment? One reason was the simple need for job security. McIntyre, the left fielder, was fast and had a good arm, but he was not a particularly strong batter. He was most at risk to lose his job to Cobb. He and his friends were determined to drive Cobb off the team before that could happen.

There were other factors as well. To his teammates, the Southern Cobb was nearly as much a foreigner as someone who had actually come from another country. Most ballplayers were from the North. Many were German and Irish Catholics, who drank, smoked, and liked to have a good time.

Cobb spoke with a difficult-to-understand Southern drawl. He did not smoke or drink. He was still small—three inches (7.6 centimeters) shorter and 35 pounds (16 kilograms) lighter than he would be at his physical peak. He was in many ways an outsider.

To the end of his days, Cobb blamed the treatment he received from his teammates for his legendary ferocity, on and off the field. "Those old-timers made a snarling wildcat out of me," he often said.

Cobb was all alone. The Tigers' manager refused to get involved in the feud. Cobb—stubborn, defiant, and full of pride—refused to back off or give in. As quoted by Al Stump, he said, "If I'd been meek and submissive and hadn't fought back, the world never would have heard of Ty Cobb."

Other players disagreed with that assessment. They thought that the hazing he received was the same as any other rookie received. They felt that with Cobb's temperament and lack of humor, he was just less able to handle it. If he had been able to laugh it off, they thought, the hazing would have ended a lot sooner. As Sam Crawford said years later, quoted in Bak's *Cobb:*

> Every rookie gets a little hazing, but most of them just take it and laugh. Cobb took it the wrong way. He came up with an antagonistic attitude, which in his mind turned any little razzing into a life-or-death struggle. He always figured everybody was ganging up on him.

Perhaps the truth lies somewhere between the two stories. In any case, it was not in Cobb's nature to take his teammates' behavior lightly. And more sensitive teammates might have realized that Cobb could not handle the hazing and backed off. Either way, the war between Cobb and his teammates continued.

On March 30, Cobb left training camp to attend his mother's trial on the charge of voluntary manslaughter. Following only seven hours of testimony and deliberation, Amanda Cobb was acquitted of the charge by an all-male jury. Cobb was incredibly relieved that his mother was not going to have to go to jail. Despite the rumors, he had found it impossible to believe that his father's killing was anything but an accident and a tragic mistake. Friends saw no evidence that he hated his mother for the killing.

Although the burden of the trial was over, Cobb was still responsible for his family's financial well-being. When William

★ ★ ★ ★ ★ ★

A BOUT WITH TONSILLITIS

Just before the 1906 season opened, Ty Cobb woke up one morning in the Boody Hotel in Toledo, Ohio. He had a 102-degree fever. His throat hurt so much that he could not swallow. The hotel doctor diagnosed him with tonsillitis.

Today, having one's tonsils removed is a safe, common, and relatively pain-free procedure. Not so in the early 1900s. As Cobb described it to Al Stump, "Putting a stranglehold on my neck, without an anesthetic, this doc cut me seven times before he was finished. Each time a piece [of tissue] came out, blood spurted and choked me. Between some of the seven cuts, I'd collapse on a sofa. He didn't seem to know what he was doing. Germany had to half-carry me back to my room, bleeding and gagging. This went on for two days." (Germany was Herman "Germany" Schaefer, a Detroit outfielder who sat with Cobb during the surgery.)

The next day, Tiger management forced Cobb to play seven innings in an exhibition game against Columbus. Weak and in pain, Cobb still managed to hit a double. He never quite forgave the team's management, though, for their insensitivity to his pain.

The next year, Cobb did some research on his doctor. He learned that, in the winter after his surgery, the doctor had been sent to live in an asylum for the insane.

Cobb died, he left his family in debt, largely because of the farm. Although the Tigers were paying Cobb about $215 a month, $100 of that was going home to Royston.

When the 1906 season finally began, Cobb spent the first week sitting on the bench. Then, Sam Crawford was injured with a pulled leg muscle. Cobb was sent in to replace him.

Unfortunately, Cobb started out in a bit of a batting slump. He also made several costly running and fielding errors. Desperate to prove himself, he started to bunt rather than go for base hits. In doing so, he was able to score runners from third base. As an added bonus, with his exceptional speed, he often got safely to first base himself.

All this time, his teammates' antagonism continued. Cobb did find a roommate with whom he could get along. His name was Edgar "Eddie" Willett, and he was a fellow Southerner. The arrangement did not last long, however. After receiving warnings from some of the other Tigers to find another roommate or "get hurt bad," Willett quit rooming with Cobb. Cobb never forgave Willett for abandoning him and not standing up to his teammates.

The conflict came to a head in a game against Chicago. A line drive went straight between Cobb in center field and McIntyre in left. When neither Cobb nor McIntyre would make a play for it, Manager Bill Armour exploded in anger. McIntyre explained to him that he would do nothing to help Cobb. With that confession, McIntyre was suspended, and Cobb began to play on a regular basis.

Cobb's batting average steadily improved. Soon, he was hitting .317. He led the team in batting as well as hitting in the clutch. With more time on base, he was able to steal more bases—11 by July. His play was getting noticed, in Detroit and nationally.

With that notice came a nickname. Joe Jackson, sportswriter for the *Detroit Free Press*, called Cobb "a peach of a player," and then "the Georgia Peach." The name soon caught on with fans.

With the flurry of publicity came additional resentment from his teammates. They were jealous of the attention that the rapidly rising star was receiving.

For his part, Cobb did nothing to try to reach out to the other players. He had given up on that possibility. He ate alone and roomed alone. Rather than go out with his teammates, he would go back to his room after a game.

There, he studied his notes on baseball. He would lay on his bed, staring up at the ceiling, working out ways that he could beat the competition. This turned out to be one of Cobb's greatest strengths as a player. He probably studied, thought about, and planned baseball plays and strategy more than any other player of his time.

But the stress of playing baseball on a team on which nobody liked him took its toll. From June 20 to July 15, his batting average dropped nearly 50 points. His fielding and running were off. He became an entirely different player. He was, in fact, quite ill.

On July 17, Cobb suddenly disappeared from public view during a series in Boston. The Tigers told the press that he had been sent back to Detroit because of stomach trouble. Reports spread that he had an ulcer. Years later, the truth was finally discovered. Ty Cobb had suffered a nervous breakdown.

In 1906, mental illness was not widely understood, but it was obvious that Cobb had been under a great deal of stress. His father's death and his mother's trial, along with the mistreatment by his teammates, had damaged Cobb mentally and physically. He had reached a breaking point. He needed to get away and rest.

Cobb was treated in a sanitarium for 44 days. While there, he was able to relax, take long walks in the woods, and not think about baseball. The truth of his condition was never released to the public. It would have been too damaging to his reputation as a tough baseball player. All anyone knew was that he had stomach problems.

Several players and coaches with the Detroit Tigers are pictured before leaving in 1908 for spring training in San Antonio, Texas. They were *(from left)* Harry Tuthill, "Bumpus" Jones, Matty McIntyre, Henry Beckendorf, Davy Jones, Ed Killian, Sam Crawford, Ed Summers, George Winter, and Hughie Jennings. Ty Cobb and his teammates were at odds almost from the start, and in his first full season, 1906, he and McIntyre seemed to be particular enemies.

Cobb returned to the Tigers' lineup on September 3. He quickly got back into the rhythm of the game. By the end of the season, he had raised his batting average back up to .320. His batting average was the best by far of anyone on the Tigers, and it was good enough to tie for fourth in the American League. Not bad for a rookie who had played only 98 games in the season. His .320 average would be the lowest that Cobb would achieve for the rest of his professional career.

Before the season ended, one more altercation occurred involving Cobb and McIntyre. Once again, a line drive went right between Cobb and McIntyre, neither of whom would make a move toward the ball. The Tigers' pitcher, Ed Siever, was furious.

After the game, in the clubhouse, Siever took a swing at Cobb, who deflected the punch. Cobb responded with a right to Siever's jaw. Siever dropped down to the ground. Rather than stopping there, Cobb continued to punch Siever, as well as kick him in the face and head. Their teammates finally broke up the fight, but not before Cobb had broken Siever's jaw.

Cobb's ferocious attack warned the anti-Cobb faction on the team that he was absolutely merciless when he fought back. It also showed a vicious streak in Cobb that would reveal itself time and time again over the coming years.

When Cobb returned to Royston for the off-season, friends noticed he had changed. He had become a loner. He was as wary and suspicious of his old friends as he was of his teammates back in Detroit. Even his oldest friend, Joe Cunningham, found himself ignored. Instead of going hunting with him, Cobb would go out on his own. He would not even talk about baseball with anyone. As Cunningham described him in Stump's *Cobb*, "Tyrus was always angry."

A Great Ballplayer

Ty Cobb was still angry when spring training began for the 1907 season. He was also feeling the financial pressure of supporting his family. His salary for the season had jumped to $2,400. An attack of boll weevils, though, had destroyed the cotton crop on his Georgia farm, driving the farm even deeper into debt.

On top of that, the feud dividing the team continued. Cobb was told that Matty McIntyre and Ed Siever refused to sign contracts with Detroit unless Cobb was off the team. Cobb himself would have been happy to be traded, but no good deals were available. He was informed by management that it was his responsibility to get along with the rest of the team. McIntyre and Siever were persuaded to sign. Tension ruled the Tigers.

Ty Cobb took part in fielding practice before a Detroit Tigers game in 1907 at Cleveland. After some violent fights during spring training, the Tigers tried to trade Cobb, but no other team wanted someone with his reputation. He went on to have a stellar season, batting .350 with 212 hits.

During spring training, one of the ugliest incidents of Cobb's career erupted. Cobb discovered that one of his four-fingered gloves was missing some fingers. He accused the groundskeeper, an African-American man named Bungy Davis, of damaging his glove. Davis denied the accusation.

Several days later, Davis tried to shake Cobb's hand and slap him on the shoulder. Cobb was still certain that Davis had cut up his glove. Also, given his upbringing as a white Southerner, he resented Davis treating him like an equal. His temper exploded into violence.

Cobb smacked Davis to the ground. He then began to kick him hard in the head. Davis somehow managed to get up and flee to a shack near the clubhouse. Cobb followed in quick pursuit.

Davis locked himself in the shack. His wife confronted Cobb, saying, according to Al Stump's *Cobb,* "Leave Bungy alone. . . . If you hurt my man, I'll have the law on you." Cobb was in a state of uncontrolled fury and could not be stopped. He knocked her to the ground and began to choke her. It took several men, including Charles "Boss" Schmidt, the Tigers' catcher and former heavyweight boxer, to drag Cobb off of her.

The next day, Tigers owner Frank J. Navin and new manager Hughie Jennings tried again to trade their troubled player to another team. Nobody wanted him. He was obviously a talented player. No team, however, wanted a man with his reputation for violence and his inability to get along with teammates. For now the Tigers would be stuck with him.

Violence broke out again on March 23. Cobb teased Charles Schmidt about his clumsiness as a catcher. Schmidt called Cobb names. A fight broke out. Cobb always claimed that Schmidt had sucker-punched him and that he never had a chance. Whoever started the fight, Cobb was no match for Schmidt, a former pro boxer who outweighed Cobb by almost 50 pounds (23 kilograms).

With most of the team watching, Schmidt pounded Cobb mercilessly. Cobb would not surrender. His mouth was cut. His eyes were swollen shut. He was covered with blood. He did not quit until he went down for the fourth time and was unable to stand back up. His teammates were happy to see him get "what he deserved." They were also impressed by and respectful of his unwillingness to give in.

THE 1907 SEASON

With Opening Day fast approaching, manager Hughie Jennings had to find some way to keep the peace. The previous year, the Tigers had come in sixth place in the American League. The fans were desperate for a winning team. Jennings would do all he could to oblige.

Since McIntyre refused to play anywhere near Cobb, Jennings began by rearranging his outfield. He put Cobb in right, McIntyre in left, and moved Sam Crawford to center field, separating the two. That way, they could keep the fighting to a minimum, at least in the outfield.

Cobb played throughout the 1907 season like a man possessed. His Opening Day play—with two hits, one stolen base, and two runs scored—was a typical Cobb performance. By the time the summer weather of June arrived (he always played better in hot weather), he was batting .350. By July, he was the first player in the majors to reach 100 hits.

He had also become a master at stealing bases. Cobb kept notes on all of the opposing pitchers and fielders, analyzing their strengths and weaknesses. He would challenge pitchers by taking long leads off of first base. This would force them to keep throwing back to first, often as many as 15 times in an inning. He would do anything and everything he could to exhaust opposing players, either physically or mentally.

Cobb developed a basic philosophy about baseball. As explained by Al Stump in his biography, *Cobb*, he felt that:

> A defensive play was at least five times as difficult to make as an offensive play. The potential was there for an unassisted fielder's error, a bad throw, a misplay from a bad hop of the ball, the shielding of the ball by the runner, and a mix-up of responsibility between two infielders or two outfielders. On offense you had fewer ways to fail after putting the ball in play. Therefore: Attack, with the confidence that the odds are with you. *Attack, attack—always attack.* Once you put the

ball in play, the defense has to retire you. Make them throw
it. Let them beat themselves with a mistake.

A fine example of this philosophy took place in a game
against the Chicago White Sox. Cobb was on second, and the
batter hit a ground ball deep toward the shortstop. Cobb ran to
third, and ignoring the sign from the third-base coach to stop,
he kept on running to home. Thinking quickly, Cobb had realized that the shortstop would have to field the ball and regain
his balance. He would then have to turn toward home plate and
position himself to make the long throw to home. Cobb figured
that the odds were in his favor—and he was right. He beat the
throw by inches.

Another example occurred during a three-game series with
the New York Highlanders. In the first game, Cobb stole home
to score the winning run. In the second game, he stole home
a second time. In the third game, the Highlanders managed to
keep Cobb from getting to base until the seventh inning. Then,
on a bunt-and-run play, Cobb made it all the way to third. The
third baseman, frustrated with himself for not tagging Cobb
out, threw the ball into the dirt. Before he knew it, Cobb, always
alert, had taken off for home. He scored again.

As Cobb explained in Bak's *Cobb*, "I was always looking
to create a mental hazard. . . . All I had to do was to make the
opposition keep on throwing the ball. Sooner or later, somebody would make a wild throw."

Indeed, Cobb made two to four attempts at stealing base
per game. His physically aggressive style of playing ball took its
toll on his body. From his ankles to his hips, his legs were covered in bloody sores. By September 1907, his legs were so sore
that he needed help to pull on his pants. Advised to stay in bed
to allow his wounds to heal, he continued to play.

The day after receiving that advice, he leaped the ropes
holding back the overflow crowd while going after a fly ball.
He made the play but cut his right hand (his throwing hand)

open from thumb to palm on a broken bottle. He bandaged his hand up and kept playing. He did not miss a single game because of his injuries, even after his hand became badly infected. His ferocious stubbornness would not allow him to be defeated by anything.

Cobb quickly became one of the most talked-about men in baseball. As cited in Stump's *Cobb*, the *New York World* editorialized, "With young Cobb there's never telling what might happen. . . . The fantastic, impossible twist is an easy possibility and we sit there like children wondering what miracle he will perform next. . . . He seems to derive unholy joy at the havoc he causes. Cobb charging home when expected to stay at third makes it more than a game—we see *drama* . . . a never-failing source of enchantment."

With Cobb leading the way, the Tigers went from sixth place in 1906 to winning the American League championship in 1907. Cobb ended the regular season batting .350 with 212 hits. He accounted for nearly one-third of the Tigers' total runs for the season. He also had 119 runs batted in and 49 stolen bases. All of these were league highs.

For his efforts, he received a diamond-studded medal for winning the batting championship. (The Most Valuable Player award had yet to be established.) He was only 20 years old. He was the youngest man to win the batting championship until Al Kaline, also of the Detroit Tigers, won it 48 years later.

During the season, Cobb signed an agreement to appear in advertisements. He endorsed a Georgia beverage that was becoming known throughout the United States—Coca-Cola. It was the beginning of a highly profitable relationship.

While Cobb and the Tigers sizzled throughout the regular season, their performance fizzled in the World Series. Facing the Chicago Cubs, they played to a tie in the first game. (In the days before electrically lighted night games, games would be declared a tie on account of darkness.) The Tigers then lost the next four games. Cobb's performance was equally dismal. He batted only .200 with just one run scored, no bases stolen, and no runs batted in.

The following season, the Tigers were once again in the hunt for the American League pennant. The race would come down to the last game of the regular season between Detroit and the Chicago White Sox. The team that won the game would win the league championship. Cobb led the way with one triple, two singles, and three runs batted in. He also forced the pitcher, "Big Ed" Walsh, into a wild throw that allowed another Tiger run to score. The Tigers won the game, 7-0.

For the second year in a row, the Tigers faced the Cubs in the World Series. And, for the second year in a row, they lost in five games, winning only one. Cobb, though, redeemed his performance of the previous year. He batted .368 against the same pitchers who had dominated him the year before. In the third game, he batted four-for-five.

His improved performance against the Cubs illustrated one of Cobb's greatest strengths as a batter. He was able to study and dissect why a particular pitcher was effective against him. Then, he could adjust his batting accordingly.

For example, batting against Doc White of the Chicago White Sox in the 1905 season, Cobb went hitless his first 13 times. Then, after figuring out how to hit against White's curveball, he raised his average against him to .387.

His scientific approach to hitting made him a remarkably consistent batter. Cobb could hit nearly anything thrown at him by either right-handed or left-handed pitchers. Fastballs, curveballs, and spitballs—he could hit them all. It did not matter whether he was playing at home or away. He rarely went more than two games without getting a hit.

This consistency led to one of his greatest accomplishments as a batter. For 23 consecutive seasons, his batting average was always better than .300.

When he did enter one of his very rare slumps, he had a strategy in place to get out of it. During batting practice, he would concentrate on bunting the ball back toward the mound. Then, he would gradually increase the arc of his swing, until finally his batting was back where he wanted it.

At the end of the 1908 season, Cobb again led the American League in batting average at .324. He also led the league in doubles (36), triples (20), and hits (188). He was the only American League player to have more than 100 runs batted in. (He had 108.) And, in a season of extraordinarily strong pitching, he was one of only three batters in the league to hit over .300.

All in all, he certainly earned the $4,000 contract he had received at the beginning of the year—plus the extra $800 he earned for winning the batting championship for the second straight season.

The 1908 season was also remarkable for another reason. On August 3, without telling anyone in the Tigers' management, he left the team to get on a train for Augusta, Georgia. The Tigers were in the middle of a tight pennant race. Management was dumbfounded that the biggest star would just walk off the team. At that point in his career, though, Cobb was too important a player to punish. The Tigers needed him more than he needed them.

But why did he leave the team? On August 6, 1908, Ty Cobb, 21 years old, married 17-year-old Charlotte "Charlie" Marion Lombard. She was a pretty, convent-educated brunette. Cobb had been courting her since she was only 14 years old. The daughter of a prominent Augusta businessman, she was heiress to a reported $300,000 fortune. At the wedding's cake ceremony, Cobb carried with him his favorite 35-ounce bat for good luck.

ANOTHER PENNANT AND MORE CONTROVERSY

The 1909 Tigers once again won the American League pennant, winning a record 98 games. Cobb, too, had a banner year, winning the coveted Triple Crown. This meant that he led the league in batting (.377), RBIs (107), and even home runs (9).

It is interesting to note that, in 1909, nine home runs were all that it took to lead the league.

Pitchers were completely stymied by Cobb. If they pitched to him, odds were pretty good that he would get a hit. Unlike many other batters, though, they could not walk him, either. If Cobb got on base, he could not be stopped.

He set a new record in 1909 with 76 stolen bases. He had, as Richard Bak pointed out, "perfected the art of pulling his body away from an infielder's tag and touching his toe into a distant corner of the base as he slid past."

As Tiger catcher Henry Beckendorf pointed out, in Bak's *Cobb*, "He is fast, and he can throw his body like an eel. You can't figure on what side he is coming. It seems as though he can throw his body while he is diving at the base. . . . I really do not think that Ty ever tried to spike a baseman intentionally. He comes in so fast and throws his body so quickly that he cannot figure on the position of the baseman."

Very few people believed that Cobb did not intentionally spike while sliding during a game against Philadelphia on August 24, 1909. The Tigers were playing a three-game series against the Athletics, who led the Tigers by one game in the standings.

In the bottom of the first inning, Cobb walked and stole second. Sam Crawford took a fourth ball for a walk, and Cobb suddenly took off running, racing toward third. The catcher easily made the throw to third baseman Frank Baker. Coming into third, Cobb faked a backslide to his left. At the same time, he whipped his right leg hard at the base. His spikes slashed Baker's forearm, which quickly began to bleed. Cobb was called safe.

Baker's wound was little more than a scratch. Indeed, he played the remainder of the game. Even the league president said that Cobb had been within his rights on the play.

The damage, though, had been done. Philadelphia sportswriters turned a minor incident into major headlines.

Ty Cobb slid into third base, trying to beat the tag from Frank Baker of the Philadelphia Athletics. On a similar play in 1909, Cobb's spikes cut Baker's arm. Baker was only slightly hurt and played the rest of the game, but Philadelphia sportswriters and fans were outraged. Cobb's reputation as a "dirty" player was growing.

Cobb's reputation as a "dirty" player began to spread, as did the myth that he sharpened his spikes to make them even more dangerous.

After he retired from baseball, Cobb always rigorously denied that he sharpened his spikes. No evidence has ever emerged that he did. While he was playing, however, Cobb saw no reason to deny the story. Any story that made fielders even more afraid of him was a story that he definitely encouraged.

Throughout his career, Cobb never apologized to anyone for how he played the game. For Cobb, baseball was more than just a game. It was serious business. As he said in his autobiography:

> When I played ball, I didn't play for fun. To me it wasn't Parcheesi played under Parcheesi rules. Baseball is a red-blooded sport for red-blooded men. It's no pink tea, and mollycoddles had better get out. It's a contest and everything that implies; a struggle for supremacy, a survival of the fittest. Every man in the game, from the minors on up, is not only fighting against the other side, but he's trying to hold on to his own job, against those on his own bench who'd love to take it away. Why deny this? Why minimize it? Why not boldly admit it?

This take-no-prisoners attitude is what helped to make Cobb a great baseball player. The same attitude—"a struggle for supremacy, a survival of the fittest"— off the field is what constantly got Cobb in trouble. His need to always prove himself as number one, as the best, as the toughest, won him very few friends.

Less than two weeks after the Baker incident, Cobb was again in the headlines. This time it involved a fight at the Hotel Euclid in Cleveland.

Arriving at the hotel late at night, Cobb was allegedly told by the night elevator man (who happened to be African American) that no elevators ran after midnight. Cobb would have to take the stairs to his room. Cobb did not like the elevator man's attitude and slapped him across the face.

The African-American night watchman, George Stansfield, approached them. A shouting match began. Stansfield took out his nightstick and whacked Cobb with it.

Cobb then pulled out a knife and slashed at Stansfield, stabbing him several times in the ear, shoulder, and hands.

Meanwhile, Stansfield kept hitting Cobb with the nightstick and managed to pull out his gun. Cobb knocked Stansfield down and kicked the gun away. He proceeded to kick Stansfield again and again in the head. At that point, the desk clerk and several janitors managed to pull Cobb off the badly injured night watchman.

Cobb retreated to his room to bandage his wounds. The next day, he refused to be benched. He played all 18 innings of a doubleheader. His bandages were stained with blood.

The Tigers made it out of Cleveland before news of the fight appeared. Lawyers for the Tigers plea-bargained Cobb's case down from a serious charge of felonious assault with intent to kill to a simple case of assault and battery. He was fined only $100. Stansfield settled his civil lawsuit against Cobb out of court for an undisclosed amount.

Cobb could thank a friendly judge and the high-powered Tiger attorneys for his lenient treatment. Even so, the case was not completely settled until November 1909. Until then, while the baseball season was still going on, Cobb made it a point to avoid traveling through Ohio to avoid possible arrest.

END OF THE 1909 SEASON

A four-game series against the Athletics began on September 16 in Philadelphia. At that point, the Tigers were only four games ahead of Philadelphia for the American League championship. The series was a critical one, and it was the first time Cobb had returned to Philadelphia since the Frank Baker spiking.

Tensions were high in Philadelphia. Cobb received death threats. People threatened to shoot him from the stands if he played. Jennings wanted to pull Cobb from the lineup, but Cobb would have none of it. He played all four games (with added police protection) without major incident. He even faced down an angry mob one evening while taking his usual stroll outside of his hotel after the game.

He did not play particularly well during the series. The Tigers still managed to win one of the four games, allowing them to maintain their lead. They would go on to win the American League championship for the third straight season.

And, for the third straight season, the Tigers lost the World Series. This time, they lost to the Pittsburgh Pirates. The Pirates were led by baseball legend Honus Wagner, the only man of that time who rivaled Cobb for the title of baseball's greatest player.

The Pirates won the series, four games to three. Unlike during the regular season, Honus Wagner outplayed Ty Cobb. His batting average for the series was .333, as opposed to Cobb's .231. Cobb was furious at losing the World Series and at being outplayed by Wagner. It would be the last time in Cobb's career that he would play in a World Series.

1910 AND THE CHALMERS AWARD

After losing the 1909 World Series, Cobb signed a three-year contract with the Tigers. The contract paid him $9,000 a year, second in the majors only to Wagner. Cobb used his salary to begin making a series of wise investments. He purchased an automobile showroom in Augusta, Georgia. He also began to buy stock in General Motors, among other companies. Because of his knack for investing wisely, Cobb would be independently wealthy within 10 years. He became known as baseball's first millionaire athlete.

Cobb enjoyed his earnings, but it was his desire to always be the best that continued to drive him. The 1910 Tigers were not a factor in the pennant race. Despite the failings of the team, Cobb's need for personal glory continued to drive him to greater and greater heights as a player. As it turned out, he was entering one of the strongest periods of his career in baseball.

The automaker Hugh Chalmers had made an announcement at the beginning of the 1910 season. He promised that the winner of the batting championship in each league would receive a new car. It would be the Chalmers "30"—a top-of-the-line automobile worth $2,700. An automobile was not the everyday item it is today. So, giving away a fine automobile as an award captured the imagination of the public.

★ ★ ★ ★ ★

AUTOMOBILES

Ty Cobb loved automobiles, and he loved speed.

In 1910, when Cobb won the Chalmers Award and a new Chalmers automobile, only a small number of Americans owned automobiles. They were still expensive and far beyond the means of most ordinary Americans. Many people, as well, thought that cars were nothing more than dangerous, unreliable machines.

How could a car possibly replace a horse? Until 1912, cars did not come with a key and electric starter. Instead, the driver had to turn a crank mounted on the outside of the car to start the engine. Using the crank took a lot of muscle (it was very difficult for most women). Also, a crank could begin to spin along with the crankshaft when the engine started. So a person could easily break an arm or jaw, or even rip his arm out of its socket in the process. And that was just to start the car.

Tires blew out frequently. Replacements were expensive. A set of new tires cost hundreds of dollars but typically lasted only a few hundred miles.

Of course, before 1909, there were virtually no paved roads anywhere in the United States. In 1909, one mile of concrete highway was laid for Woodland Avenue in Detroit. It was the first concrete road anywhere in the country.

Most roads were little better than dirt. Rain or snow made them nearly impassable. It's no wonder then that people, seeing a car broken down or stuck in the mud, would shout, "Get a horse!"

In the National League, the car went to Philadelphia Phillies outfielder Sherry Magee without too much of a contest. In the American League, though, the competition between Ty Cobb and Cleveland's Napoleon "Nap" Lajoie continued for the entire season. As you may recall, back in 1903, 16-year-old Ty traveled to Atlanta to watch his idol Lajoie play baseball. Now, just seven years later, he was battling with him for the American League batting championship.

At the beginning of September, Cobb led Lajoie by only three percentage points. Throughout September and into October, the lead seesawed between the two. By October 6, Cobb led Lajoie by eight percentage points. Cobb wanted the car. Not willing to take any chances at losing his lead, he sat out the last two games of the season.

This strategy had a few problems. One was that the eight-point lead was unofficial. Without computers and today's technology, recordkeeping was much less precise than it is now. Different newspapers and different sportswriters calculated batting averages in various ways. It was so confusing that the offices of the American League declared that "the result probably will not be known until [league secretary] Rob McRoy gives out his figure."

The other problem was Cobb's unpopularity in comparison to Lajoie's popularity. Fights and violence had continued in Cobb's life. He had slapped an African-American waiter across the face for bringing him the wrong order. He had charged into the stands to attack an abusive fan.

Few players wanted Cobb to win, but many, many players rooted for Lajoie. As it turned out, some players hated Cobb so much that they were willing to do almost anything to help Lajoie come out on top.

Cleveland's last two games of the regular season were a doubleheader against the last-place St. Louis Browns. The Browns were managed by Jack O'Connor, who was known to hate Cobb.

Ty Cobb did enjoy his automobiles. During the 1910 season, he and Napoleon Lajoie battled back and forth in the race for the batting title. Automaker Hugh Chalmers was going to give a new car to the winner of the batting championship. In the end, the finish was close and disputed, so Chalmers awarded an auto to each player.

On orders from O'Connor, whenever Lajoie came to bat, third baseman Red Corriden played him too far back. It was impossible for Corriden to make easy plays when Lajoie hit bunts up the third baseline. At other times, fielders misplayed easy hits, or made wild throws to base. Lajoie ended the double-header with eight hits in eight times at bat.

The eight-for-eight performance should have been enough to win Lajoie the championship. Even eight players from the Tigers, including Matty McIntyre, Sam Crawford, and Davy Jones, sent Lajoie a telegram congratulating him on his victory. You know you are disliked when your own teammates congratulate someone on an opposing team for beating you.

The congratulations turned out to be premature. Members of the press were outraged by the St. Louis Browns' obvious cheating. An investigation took place. After much discussion, the fraudulent eight hits were included in Lajoie's final statistics. Cobb, too, was given credit for one additional single that had been previously scored as a fielder's error.

It took one week to declare the winner. Napoleon Lajoie's final batting average was .384084. Ty Cobb's was .384944. Cobb had won by the slimmest of margins. In a spirit of generosity, Chalmers declared both men to be winners and awarded each of them a car.

The Browns were punished for their attempt to help Lajoie win the batting championship. Ban Johnson, the American League president, forced St. Louis management to fire manager Jack O'Connor and coach Harry Howell. They never worked in Major League Baseball again.

THE 1911 SEASON

Cobb showed off his mastery of the psychological aspects of the game during the 1911 season. He had been having one of his best seasons to date as a batter. He had even had one streak during which he had at least one hit in 40 straight games. Incredibly, though, by the end of the season, another player,

"Shoeless" Joe Jackson, was leading him in batting average by nine points.

The Tigers had a six-game series against Jackson's Cleveland Naps in Cleveland. Before this series, Cobb and Jackson, both Southerners, had been friendly on and off the field. Cobb used this friendship to get inside Jackson's head.

As Cobb recalled in his autobiography, during the six days of the series, whenever Jackson tried to talk to him, Cobb would ignore him. At other times, he would yell at Jackson for no apparent reason. Jackson began to wonder what he had done to upset Cobb.

As quoted in his autobiography, Cobb said, "My mind was concentrated on one thing: Getting all the base hits I could muster. Joe Jackson's mind was on many other things. He went hitless in the first three games of the series, while I fattened up. By the sixth game, I'd passed him in the averages." As soon as the series ended, of course, Cobb resumed talking to Jackson as if nothing had ever happened.

A new, livelier, cork-centered ball had been introduced in 1911. The advantage it gave to hitters was apparent in the increased batting averages, hits, and home runs. Jackson ended the season with a batting average of .408. Cobb ended it with a .420 average, for his fifth batting title in a row. He also ended the season with 248 hits, 147 runs scored, 127 RBIs, and 83 stolen bases—all league bests. He also led the league in doubles, triples, and slugging percentage.

One statistic alone demonstrates how successful he was as a batter. In the entire 1911 season, he struck out swinging only twice. For his efforts, he was selected to receive the 1911 Chalmers Award, which was now being given to the man considered the most valuable player, not just the winner of the batting title.

One of Cobb's games against the New York Highlanders (they would officially become known as the Yankees in 1913) is a great example of his accomplishments during the season. He

In 1911, Ty Cobb was again involved in a fight for the batting title—this time with his friend "Shoeless" Joe Jackson *(right)*, who played for Cleveland. During one series with Cleveland toward the end of the season, Cobb ignored or yelled at Jackson, making Jackson wonder what he had done to anger Cobb. As a result, Jackson's batting suffered, and Cobb went on to win the title.

scored one run running from first base on a single to right field. He scored another run from second base on a wild pitch. In the seventh inning, he tied up the game with a two-run double. The catcher for the Highlanders disagreed with a call and began to argue with the umpire.

The argument became so heated that other Highlander fielders moved in closer so they could see and hear what was going on. Since the game was still being played (no one had called time), Cobb moved from second to third. He then slowly moved toward home, making it look as if he wanted to see the continuing argument. He then suddenly ran and slid safely into home with the winning run.

Nobody in baseball, before or since, has played the game quite like Ty Cobb.

The Greatest Player Who Ever Lived?

Ty Cobb continued his domination of the game in 1912, winning his sixth straight batting title with an average of .410. What is remembered most about the 1912 season, though, was a fight he had with Claude Lucker.

Lucker was a loudmouthed fan of the New York Highlanders. He enjoyed nothing more than shouting insults at opposing players. He hated no opposing player more than Ty Cobb.

On May 15, 1912, Lucker was sitting about 12 rows behind the visitors' dugout in the Yankees' old stadium, Hilltop Park. From the moment the game began, Lucker shouted insults at Cobb.

Cobb answered every insult with an insult of his own, but he tried to avoid a physical confrontation. Lucker continued to shower Cobb with insults and foul language. He shouted horrible things about Cobb's mother. Finally, he called Cobb a racial epithet. Racial insults were unfortunately much more common then than they are today. Using one against Ty Cobb, given his feelings about African Americans, was possibly the worst thing Lucker could have said.

Cobb climbed up into the stands and attacked Lucker. He hit him in the face with his fists, knocking him down. He proceeded to kick him, hitting him with his spikes on the lower half of his body. Finally, the police dragged Cobb away. What Cobb did not realize in his fury was that Lucker was unable to strike back.

In an accident at work, Lucker had lost one of his hands as well as three fingers off the other hand. Cobb had given a ruthless beating to a physically helpless and defenseless man.

Cobb was tossed from the game and suspended for an indefinite period of time. An interesting thing happened, though. Many of the nation's newspapers, along with Cobb's own teammates, took Cobb's side in the fight.

Cobb was still widely disliked, but they felt that Lucker's insults were more than any man should have to take. They felt that Cobb, by fighting Lucker, was merely defending his honor as a man. As baseball writer Hugh Fullerton said in Bak's *Cobb*, "If the epithets and accusations made by the . . . fan toward Cobb were half as bad as the Detroit players claim, it was a case for violence."

For the first and maybe the last time in his career, Cobb had the support of all his teammates. They sent a telegram to Ban Johnson, the American League president. They stated that Cobb had been within his rights to do what he did. Because of this, they said, they would not play baseball as long as Cobb was on suspension. For the first time in baseball history, a team had gone on strike.

The strike lasted exactly one game. In that game, Detroit put up a substitute team made up of college and amateur

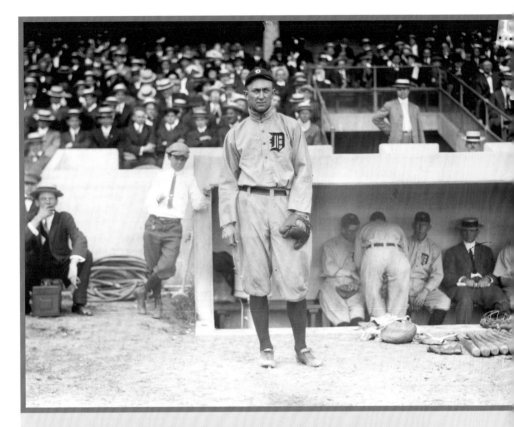

Ty Cobb watched the action during a game in 1913. His fame as a baseball player was at its peak. In the previous two seasons, Cobb batted over .400, and he would hit .390 in 1913. Still, fights with fans and other skirmishes off the field continued to mar his reputation.

players against the Philadelphia Athletics. The substitute team lost, 24-2. Cobb then urged his teammates to get back out and play baseball. They did, and Cobb's suspension was ended after only 10 games.

Cobb's contract with the Tigers ended in 1912. Despite his ongoing problems with violent behavior, he was still the Tigers' star player. He knew that he deserved another large pay increase. He demanded that his salary be raised to $15,000 per season for three years.

The Tigers' owner, Frank Navin, refused to meet Cobb's demands. Cobb held out when the season started. A new contract was not agreed upon until late April 1913, giving Cobb $12,000 for one year. Once again, Cobb won the batting title with a major-league-best .390 average. More money soon followed. In 1914, he signed a one-year contract guaranteeing him $15,000. The following year, he signed a three-year contract for $20,000 per year.

He was at the peak of his fame as a baseball player. Besides his salary with the Tigers, he earned large fees endorsing various commercial products. Among the many products he endorsed were underwear, suspenders, chewing gum, Coca-Cola, and cigarettes. He even had a nickel candy bar named after him.

This large income helped him to support his rapidly growing family. He and his wife, Charlie, would have five children: Tyrus Cobb, Jr., born in 1910, daughter Shirley in 1911, son Herschel in 1916, daughter Beverly in 1918, and son Jimmy in 1921.

Cobb loved his children but did not see them very often. During the season, he was on the road much of the time. During the off-season, he frequently traveled on business as well as played golf and took hunting trips.

He was known to be a strict father. Sometimes, too, he would (like any father) take the frustrations of his work home with him. He also had high expectations for his children. Cobb did not hesitate to let them know when they had disappointed him. Unfortunately for his wife and children, he could no more control his temper at home than he could anywhere else.

On occasion, his temper blew up while defending his family. In July 1912, Ty and Charlie were driving to the train station in Detroit. Suddenly three men jumped onto the car's running board. One man had a knife and slashed Ty. Cobb managed to pull out his pistol and chased one of the men down a dark alley. Furious, he pistol-whipped the man across his face and head again and again and again. Cobb later said

Humorist Will Rogers *(left)* explained one of his rope tricks to Ty Cobb's son, Tyrus, Jr., as Cobb watched. Cobb loved his children, but as a pro baseball player, he was away from home much of the time.

that he killed the man and left his body there in the alley. His claim has never been proven one way or another.

Another major incident occurred in June 1914. During a dinner party in Detroit, Charlie told Ty about an argument she had had with the owner of a butcher shop, William Carpenter. She claimed that Carpenter sold her 20 cents worth of spoiled fish. Carpenter denied it, insisting that the fish was fresh when it was delivered to Mrs. Cobb.

Ty phoned the butcher shop. Then, convinced that his wife (and through her, Ty himself) had been insulted, he left the party and his guests for the butcher shop, pistol in hand. When he got there, he forced Carpenter at gunpoint to call his wife and apologize.

While this was happening, another worker at the shop, Harold Harding (who was African American), tried to defend Carpenter. Cobb, almost insane with anger, hit Harding with the handle of the pistol three times in the head. He then smashed the glass cases and furniture in the shop.

Cobb forced Harding to go outside and fight. There, he continued to beat up the young man. Carpenter called the police, and Cobb was hauled off to jail for the night. Cobb eventually pleaded guilty to "disturbing the peace." For his punishment, he paid a fine of just $50. He also promised the judge that he would never do it again.

Although the court was forgiving, his other punishments were more severe. His wife, Charlie, was so humiliated by such incidents that she and the children spent most of the year in their Augusta, Georgia, home. There, they could avoid the spotlight of Cobb's continuous bad publicity.

His season with the Tigers was damaged as well. During the fight, Cobb fractured his thumb and had to sit on the bench for 52 days. Before that, the Tigers had a chance of winning the pennant. Without Cobb playing, they rapidly dropped out of contention.

When he came back on August 7, his playing ability was undiminished. He ended the season with a .368 average, enough to win another batting title—his eighth straight.

In 1915, the Tigers were once again contenders for the pennant. Despite a record of 100 wins and 54 losses, they were beaten by the Boston Red Sox with a record of 101 and 50. Finishing second was a major disappointment for Cobb and his team.

One of the newest stars on the Red Sox was a young pitcher named Babe Ruth. In 1915, his first full season, he had a pitching record of 18-8. He also hit four home runs—more than anyone else on his team. It was a faint sign of what was to come.

Cobb was disappointed at not winning the pennant, but it was a season of great personal achievements. Once again, he led the league in batting, with an average of .369—his ninth consecutive batting title. (The next-best hitter was Eddie Collins at .332.) He also led the league in scoring (144 runs) and hits (208). The 1915 season was also his best as a base stealer, with 96. This mark would stand as the major-league record for nearly 50 years. Maury Wills of the Los Angeles Dodgers finally broke the record in 1962.

Cobb had spent the winter preparing to set an unbeatable record in stolen bases. He had had a leather worker install weights in his shoes. All winter, and throughout spring training, he wore the shoes everywhere he went. Each shoe was loaded with a 10-ounce weight. When Opening Day arrived and he removed the weights, his legs were stronger than ever, and his feet felt that much lighter. He was unstoppable.

In 1915, he even stole home plate a remarkable six times. To put that in perspective, Lou Brock and Rickey Henderson ultimately surpassed Cobb in total stolen bases, but each only stole home seven times.

Over his career, Cobb stole home 54 times in regular-season play. That achievement and his career batting average of .367 are records that will probably never be surpassed.

In 1916, the Tigers lost out on the pennant again, finishing four games behind the Boston Red Sox. Something else happened that season, however, that brought even greater disappointment to Cobb.

For the first time in 10 years, Cobb was not the American League batting champion. Despite a fine average of .371, he was bested by Tris Speaker with a .386 average. Cobb swore that would never happen again.

He recaptured the batting title the following year. In 1917, he hit .383, which was 30 points higher than anyone else in the

In 1918, a season shortened because of World War I, Ty Cobb won his eleventh batting title. After the season was over, he served for three months as a captain in the U.S. Army's Chemical Warfare Service. Here, he is pictured in his captain's uniform.

majors. He also led everyone else in hits, doubles, triples, total bases, and slugging percentage.

Also in 1917, he led the league in stolen bases for the last time, with 55. Cobb was 30 years old, and his legs were starting to wear out. His speed and power as a runner were diminishing. The next year, 1918, he had only 34 steals. His numbers continued to gradually drop for the remaining 10 years of his career.

His skills as a batter, though, were undiminished. In 1918, the baseball season ended one month earlier than normal because of World War I. Still, Cobb won his eleventh batting championship, with a .382 average. And, at season's end, at the age of 31, he enlisted in the military.

He served only three months as a captain in the U.S. Army's Chemical Warfare Service. He arrived in France only three weeks before the armistice was signed to end the war. He took the first troop ship back to the United States, arriving on December 16, 1918. Cobb was almost 32 and tired. He was unsure if he wanted to continue to play baseball. He ultimately ended up signing another $20,000 contract with the Tigers. Unbeknownst to Cobb, however, the game of baseball was about to change in ways he would never appreciate.

BABE RUTH AND THE LONG BALL

As the 1919 season began, Cobb was on the verge of becoming a very wealthy man. The previous year, he had borrowed $10,800 and purchased his first 300 shares of Coca-Cola stock. The investment was one of the wisest he ever made. When he died in 1961, his Coca-Cola stock alone was valued at almost $2 million.

He returned to the game in 1919 with renewed energy. For the twelfth and final time in his career, he won the American League batting title, with an outstanding .384 average. He also produced 161 runs.

For all of his accomplishments, though, Cobb was not the main baseball story of 1919. The most talked-about player of

1919 was George Herman Ruth of the Boston Red Sox—the Babe. He had set a new record for home runs in a single season with 29.

The following year was to be even better for the Babe. During the off-season, he was sold by the Red Sox to the New York Yankees. (This deal was supposedly the beginning of the curse of the Red Sox, which did not end until their World Series victory in 2004.) At the time, the Yankees played in the Polo Grounds, a perfect stadium for a power hitter like Ruth. Now

★ ★ ★ ★ ★

TY COBB THE ACTOR

Ty Cobb liked to stay busy, and he liked to make money. He also wanted to stay in the public eye, even during the off-season. These needs drove him to try acting. Not once, but twice.

In 1911, Cobb was offered $10,000 to tour and star in the stage comedy *The College Widow*. The offer was not uncommon. Many ballplayers earned big dollars performing in vaudeville or in the theater. Cobb had never acted before, but coaching was promised. He agreed to do it.

Cobb starred as Bill Bolton, a college football hero. Reviewers were mostly kind, but people were not coming out to see a good actor in a good play. Crowds flocked to see a baseball star on stage. Cobb hated the experience.

The work was much harder than he had thought it would be. He felt uncomfortable kissing his co-star. He hated not being the best at whatever it was he was doing. And, he worried that the bright stage lights would harm his eyesight. After just six weeks, he walked out on his contract.

playing in the outfield rather than pitching, he was able to play every day.

There was more. The 1920 season saw the end of the Dead Ball Era. Before this, one ball generally lasted an entire game. By the middle of a game, the ball had softened to the point that it was no longer perfectly round. Hitting for power became nearly impossible.

Starting in 1920, the ball was replaced several times during a game. Not only that, but trick pitches like the spitball and the

He tried acting just one more time. In 1917, the Sunbeam Motion Picture Company offered him $25,000 to star in a movie entitled *Somewhere in Georgia*. The script was by the sportswriter Grantland Rice. The money was too much for Cobb to turn down. He accepted the offer. By doing so, he became the first professional athlete to star in a Hollywood film, according to Al Stump's *Cobb*.

He probably should have turned down the money. Although the role was a familiar one (he played a bank clerk who is signed by the Detroit Tigers), the plot was completely ridiculous. In the film, after being hazed by the players, his character tries to return home to Atlanta. Before he can get there, he is kidnapped, tied up, and left in a barn to die. Fortunately, he escapes and makes it home just in time to hit a home run for his town's team and marry his hometown girlfriend.

The critics were not kind. Ward Morehouse called it "absolutely the worst flicker [movie] I ever saw." The $25,000 that Cobb earned made up for the film's reception. Cobb, though, never acted again.

emery ball were basically outlawed. These changes were ideal for hitters like Babe Ruth.

Ruth's 1920 season was one that had never been seen in baseball history. He hit 54 home runs and batted .376. He led the league in runs (158), RBIs (137), and bases on balls (150). His slugging percentage of .849 was a major-league record that would last more than 80 years. It was finally beaten by Barry Bonds in 2001. (Slugging percentage measures a hitter's power. It is calculated as the total bases divided by at-bats.)

To put Ruth's achievement in perspective, his 54 home runs for the season were more than the total that any *team* in the league hit for the entire season.

Cobb, on the other hand, had a relatively disappointing year. He had had a knee injury and batted only .334—his worst performance at bat since 1906.

Ty Cobb and Babe Ruth were almost perfect opposites, on and off the field. Cobb, despite his personal failings, took baseball very seriously. He trained hard and kept himself in good shape. He believed in a methodical style of baseball. Go for hits, either singles or doubles. Steal bases. Drive runs home. It was not necessarily thrilling, but it got the job done.

Ruth changed the way baseball was played. He tended to be fat and did not take training seriously. He was known for his love of food, women, and parties. Unlike Cobb, he was loved on and off the field. Baseball fans adored him. They loved his larger-than-life personality. And, they loved watching him hit home run after home run. He changed the game from one of strategy and steady progress to one of power. The ability to hit home runs became the way great players were defined. Cobb despised this new way of play.

But baseball fans loved it, and attendance soared. People enjoyed the drama of watching Ruth come up to bat and then—wham—knock the ball out of the park. Compared to that, Cobb's style of play seemed boring and old-fashioned.

For the remainder of his career, Cobb played in the shadow of Ruth. He resented and disliked Ruth. He could not understand why the fans loved Ruth, since he was out of shape and did not play "traditional" baseball.

Tired of seeing his fame eclipsed by the Babe, he decided to make a point. On May 5, 1925, he went to speak to a reporter. Cobb told him that he was going to start to swing for the fences.

That day, Cobb went six for six, with two singles, a double, and three home runs. His 16 total bases in one game set a new American League record that still stands. The next day, he had three more hits, two of which were home runs. He had nine straight hits and five home runs in just two days.

At the end of the series, the 38-year-old Cobb went back to his style of baseball: bunting, hitting, and running. He had made his point. If he had wanted to play ball like Ruth, he could have. He chose not to.

PLAYER-MANAGER

At the end of the 1920 season, Cobb was once again at a career crossroads. He was feeling overshadowed by Ruth. The Tigers had ended up in seventh place. They showed little hope of improving over the next season. Why go on playing?

In November, he received a phone call from Tigers owner Frank Navin. He told Cobb that longtime Tigers manager Hughie Jennings had been fired. He asked Cobb if he would be interested in taking over as the new manager.

Cobb's first impulse was to say no. The added pressure of managing a team was not a task he was eager to take on. Friends and members of the media, though, pressed him to take the job. Cobb began to reconsider. He thought that by playing and managing, he would take the spotlight away from Ruth. Also, should the Tigers start winning, it would be one more major accomplishment in his career.

He took the job, along with a raise to $32,500. He was the highest-paid player in baseball. Fans in Detroit were delighted. They thought that, since he was a great ballplayer, he would automatically be a great manager as well.

Unfortunately for the Tigers, his managerial skills did not quite equal his skills as a player. He drove his players as hard as he drove himself. His tough management style could be effective. The players, though, who had never really liked him, grew to dislike him even more.

The Tigers' 1921 season was nearly as bad as their 1920 season. They did manage to improve enough to place sixth in the American League. The team was still weak in pitching and fielding. Their batting, however, improved vastly under Cobb's tutelage.

The team's batting average was an astonishing .316—the highest team average in modern baseball history. With Cobb's coaching, outfielder Harry Heilmann won the American League batting championship, with an average of .394. Who came in second? None other than Cobb himself, batting .389. He also scored 124 runs and had 22 stolen bases.

Babe Ruth still dominated the league, though, hitting a record 59 home runs, with 177 runs and 171 RBIs. Ruth dominated Cobb himself in a game against the Tigers on June 13, 1921. Ruth returned to pitching, hit two home runs, and even struck out Cobb on the way to an 11-8 Yankee victory. You can imagine Cobb's feelings about his rival after that game.

The following year, 1922, was a bad year for Ruth. Too much partying, gambling, and late nights took their toll. He also faced a six-week suspension for breaking a league rule against playing in exhibition games. At the end of the season, his numbers had dropped dramatically in every category.

Cobb, on the other hand, had a great year, both as a player and a manager. The Tigers, after a slow start, climbed up to third place in the standings, with a record of 79–75. The team's batting average was .305—18 points higher than the pennant-winning New York Yankees.

For the third time in his career, at the age of 35, Cobb batted over .400, ending the season at .401. He also scored 99 runs and had 99 RBIs. At an age when most ballplayers were close to retirement, his season was a truly remarkable achievement.

His personal life was a different matter. Relations with his wife, Charlie, were at an all-time low. In July 1921, she nearly died giving birth to their fifth child, James "Jimmy" Hull Cobb. Cobb had not been there for the delivery. He managed to make it home for just a few days during her slow recovery before returning to Detroit. Charlie felt scared and abandoned by her husband. She felt that to Ty, she and the family would always be second in importance to baseball. She began to consider divorce.

The 1923 season was another good one for the Tigers. Despite bad pitching (the team had a 4.09 ERA—second worst in the league) and sloppy fielding (103 double plays, fewest in the league) the Tigers still ended up in second place. As Al Stump put it in *Cobb*, "The 1923 season went into the records as the Georgian's finest managerial experience, the product of his willpower, seizing opportunities, and playing dirty tricks."

The "dirty tricks" included such moves as the one pulled against New York Yankees pitcher Carl Mays. Three years earlier, in 1920, Mays had hit Cleveland batter Ray Chapman with a pitch. Chapman later died of a skull fracture. Mays remained haunted by the tragedy.

When the Tigers faced Mays in 1923, Cobb had special instructions for batter Fred Haney. He instructed Haney to crowd close to the plate on his first time up to bat. If Mays's first pitch was close, Haney was to fall to the ground and pretend that he had been hit.

He did as instructed, and Cobb called for a time-out. Cobb walked out to the mound to talk to Mays. According to Al

Ty Cobb posed for a photograph in the Tigers' dugout in 1925. In 1921, Cobb became player-manager for the Tigers. As manager, he demanded as much of his players as he did of himself. During the 1920s, Babe Ruth and power hitting became popular, but Cobb was no fan of this style of ball.

Stump, all Cobb said to him was, "Now, Mr. Mays, you should be more careful where you throw. Remember Chapman?" The incident shook up Mays so badly that the Tigers won the game easily.

Tricks like that did not help Cobb's reputation. His reputation was hurt even more by incidents such as one in Philadelphia. There, Cobb punched an African-American groundskeeper for using a telephone when he needed to use it.

Another ugly incident occurred in 1924. When a waitress in a restaurant in Atlanta gave him his bill, Cobb yelled that it was $1.50 too much. Cobb tore up the check and began to curse at the restaurant staff. He was so out of control that the cashier hit him over the head with a glass platter.

When the police arrived, Cobb was still raging. He knocked out one policeman with a punch to the head. The other policeman finally overpowered him, and Cobb was taken away in a paddy wagon to the station. There, once he settled down, he was finally released. No charges were ever filed.

Cobb was definitely not mellowing with age. If anything, his tantrums were getting more violent and more out of control. The pressures of trying to manage the team, of trying to outplay Ruth, combined with all of his personal problems, were too much for him.

The pressures, though, did not affect his playing. In 1923, despite back pain so bad that he sometimes needed help to tie his shoes, he ended the season with a .340 average. On top of that, on May 25, he scored his 1,741st career run, beating out Honus Wagner's record. On September 20, he beat out Wagner again, with his 3,431st base hit.

The Tigers' last chance for a pennant under Cobb's management came in 1924. In June, they were in first place. Given their lack of quality pitching (Cobb always blamed Navin for not spending the money to get top pitchers), they soon faded. They ended the season in third place.

Many people believed that, if he had allowed the Tigers to hit for home runs rather than singles and doubles, they could have won the championship. Cobb refused to change his style, though. As always, he hated the new style of power hitting. His inability to alter his management style may have been to the detriment of the team as a whole.

As a player, though, Cobb was unstoppable. Driven by his desire for one last chance at the World Series, he played in every one of the team's 155 games. He batted .338 and stole 23 bases. He also led all American League outfielders in fielding. He made only six errors the entire season. In his late 30s, he could still outplay most men at the peak of their careers.

At the same time, a re-evaluation was taking place among sportswriters. They began to write that Babe Ruth was the undisputed home run king. But, they added, Cobb was still the better all-around player, both offensively and defensively. (Case in point, over their careers, Ruth struck out 1,330 times. Cobb struck out only 357 times, and he had more than 3,000 at-bats than Ruth.)

In the 1925 and 1926 seasons, the Tigers failed to live up to their accomplishments of 1924. They came in fourth place in 1925 and sixth in 1926. Cobb's play, too, was beginning to show signs of slipping. Plagued by injuries, exhausted by his dual role as manager and player, he played in just 121 games, ending the 1925 season batting .378. In 1926, with eye surgery at the beginning of the season, and ongoing leg injuries throughout, he only played in 79 games, hitting .339.

More than 20 years of major-league baseball were taking their toll. Also, Tigers fans were disappointed at the lack of championships. Fans were actually booing Cobb at home in Detroit. Finally, he had enough. On November 3, 1926, Cobb announced his resignation from the Detroit Tigers.

He left with a record of 3,902 hits in 2,805 games and a .369 batting average. He had scored 2,087 runs and had 1,804 RBIs, 865 stolen bases, and 12 batting championships.

Final Innings

At the same time that Ty Cobb retired, so did star player Tris Speaker of the Cleveland Indians. People were struck by the fact that two major players would retire at the same time. Was there something going on that nobody knew about?

It turned out that there was. Accusations had been made in 1926 by a former Tigers pitcher named Dutch Leonard. He claimed that Cobb and Speaker had been involved in fixing a game in 1919. This was a serious accusation, alleging that Cobb and Speaker had worked together beforehand to determine which of their teams would win the game. Such collusion would allow friends who were gambling on the game to make money. The baseball commissioner, Judge Kenesaw Mountain Landis, pushed Cobb and Speaker to retire from

Ty Cobb *(left)* and Tris Speaker became teammates on the Philadelphia Athletics in 1928. Two years earlier, both were accused by a former player of fixing a game, but the baseball commissioner found no evidence against them. The 1928 season would be Cobb's last in the major leagues.

baseball, pending investigation. That was the real reason for their resignations.

The accusation came to nothing. Leonard was unable to convince the commissioner that the two had done anything serious enough to deserve being kicked out of baseball. Some historians say that Leonard made the accusations to get back at Cobb. While managing the Tigers, Cobb had sold Leonard from the Tigers to the Pacific Coast League.

Cleared of any wrongdoing, Cobb was free to return to the Tigers if he wished. Instead, he signed to play with the Philadelphia Athletics, managed by the legendary Connie Mack. Cobb wanted a change from Detroit. Detroit wanted a change from him. The Athletics were contenders for the pennant. Besides, by coming back to play, he could get vindication for the Dutch Leonard affair. He could then leave baseball when *he* wanted to, on his own terms.

Cobb played two seasons with the Athletics. Promises of an appearance by the A's in the World Series were meaningless in 1927, the year of the New York Yankees. That year, the Yankees were at their peak, winning 110 regular-season games. They went on to sweep the Pittsburgh Pirates in four games to win the World Series. That was also the year that Babe Ruth hit 60 home runs—a record that would stand until Roger Maris hit 61 homers in 1961.

For Cobb, though, 1927 did allow him the personal vindication that he sought. No longer managing, he was able to concentrate on his play. Making adjustments for his age, he would stay in bed until noon. He would eat breakfast in bed and make his phone calls and business transactions in bed. He would not get out of bed until it was time to go to the park and play. After the game, he took long showers and then spent his evenings resting in his hotel room. There, he would read and listen to musicians like the classical violinist Fritz Kreisler on his record player.

By saving his energy for game time, he was able to play 134 games that season. He batted .357 (fifth best in the league) with 104 runs scored, 93 RBIs, and 22 stolen bases. In 490 at-bats, he struck out only 12 times. Not bad for the oldest everyday player in the majors.

In 1927, Cobb also became the first player in baseball to reach 4,000 hits. To make the occasion even sweeter, he did it while playing the Tigers in Detroit. The fans cheered Cobb, even though he was technically "the enemy." He had become, at least among Detroit fans, a beloved institution.

Fans and baseball writers alike were beginning to realize that they were witnessing the end of an era. When Cobb stopped playing, his style of ball would be no more. Many were sad to see it end. In Richard Bak's *Cobb*, he quotes baseball writer Joe Williams reporting a classic Cobb moment during a game against the Yankees:

> Ty Cobb went around the bases in the sixth inning . . . but more enlightening was the method he used—old fashioned stuff scorned in the Era of Ruth.
>
> He laid down a bunt, perfectly, which caught third baseman Joe Dugan totally by surprise. Cobb slid into first, beating Dugan's hasty throw. How long since you've seen a first base slide?
>
> Next, when Hale hit a short rap to center field, and when any-one else would have stopped at second, Cobb pumped his aged legs and went for third. Combs' throw to Dugan had him out cold. Locating the ball with a quick glance over his shoulder, Cobb slid left, then contorted himself to the right. There was a geyser of dust and when it cleared, he was seen to have half-smothered the throw with his body; as Dugan scrambled for the ball, Cobb was up and dusting himself off.
>
> The whole sequence was beautiful to see, a subtle, forgotten heritage from the romantic past.

Many thought that Cobb would retire at the end of the 1927 season. He decided to play one more season.

He probably should not have. His reflexes were slowing down. His eyesight was beginning to go. His legs were giving out. On July 27, 1928, Cobb was hit in the chest by a pitch. At the age of 41, this injury, on top of his other injuries, sent him to the bench through September. On September 11, 1928, Cobb had his last at-bat as a major leaguer, hitting a weak fly ball for an easy out.

Cobb ended the season with a .323 average, having played only 95 games. Only nine other American Leaguers had a higher average. He had also, at the age of 41, stolen home plate for the last time. He could retire with his head held high.

On September 17, 1928, Ty Cobb officially retired from baseball with 3,035 games, 11,429 at-bats, 4,191 hits, and 2,245 total runs. His career batting average of .367 has never been bettered. During his career, he set an astonishing 123 records. He was the most consistent player the game has ever known.

Baseball had been all he had ever known. It was all he had ever done, all he had ever loved. Cobb was only 41 years old. What would he do for the rest of this life?

A SLOW FADE

Cobb retired from baseball a wealthy man. His place in base-ball history was secure. He should have been a happy man. Instead, he was a lonely one.

He had few friends outside of the people he did business with. He had spent little time with his family, and they were somewhat afraid of him.

As a father Cobb could be kind and affectionate on occa-sion. But he was as demanding of his children as he was of himself. He wanted them to become great athletes and baseball players. Children, however, do not always grow up to become what their parents want.

His oldest son, Tyrus Cobb, Jr., hated baseball. He was, though, an excellent tennis player. Cobb was not happy about that. He did not consider tennis to be a "manly" enough sport for any son of his.

★ ★ ★ ★ ★

THE RUTH CUP

Even after retirement, Ty Cobb's rivalry with Babe Ruth continued. After leaving baseball, Cobb took up the game of golf. Unfortunately, he was not as good at it as he hoped to be. As you can imagine, when Cobb played badly, his temper flared. His bad behavior forced him to resign from several clubs.

In June 1941, Cobb was challenged to play Ruth in a three-game series. The money would go to charity. Cobb initially declined. Ruth was, on paper at least, a much better player. He could easily drive the ball 300 yards (274 meters). Cobb could not stand the thought of being beaten by his longtime rival. When he received a telegram from Ruth (as quoted in Al Stump's biography), however, he could not say no. "IF YOU WANT TO COME HERE AND GET YOUR BRAINS KNOCKED OUT, COME AHEAD. SIGNED, RUTH." Cobb could not resist the challenge.

Cobb was 54 years old to Ruth's 46. Cobb won the first match, but only after rattling Ruth by constantly taunting him about his weight. Ruth came back to win the second match.

For the tiebreaker, Cobb took no chances. He hired the golf course's assistant pro to be his caddie. He brought in golf champion Walter Hagen as his coach. As final insurance, he made sure that Ruth drank plenty of Scotch on his way to the match. Of course, Cobb won.

He was so proud of beating Ruth that the trophy he won from the series shared space on the same mantle as his Hall of Fame plaque.

Babe Ruth patted Ty Cobb's head after the second golf match in their three-match charity showdown in 1941. Cobb made sure Ruth had some Scotch before the third match and went on to win the tourney. Cobb got great pleasure from the victory over his longtime rival.

In late spring of 1929, Cobb received word that Tyrus had flunked out of Princeton University. He went to visit him, as well as to punish him. Pulling a bullwhip out of his bag, he whipped young Tyrus until he was bleeding.

Tyrus, Jr., transferred to Yale, where he became captain of the tennis team. In 1930, he was twice charged with drunkenness and did not graduate. Cobb provided his son with the lawyers needed to help him out legally. He then told his son that their relationship was over. There would be no more communication between father and son.

Cobb meant it. He did not speak to his son until 1952, just before Tyrus, Jr., died of a malignant brain tumor. Cobb's anger and disappointment with his son overwhelmed his love for him, keeping him from having any relationship with him.

His marriage with Charlie was in trouble as well. In 1931, she filed for divorce. Cobb persuaded her to change her mind, and the family moved from Georgia to Atherton, California, just outside of San Francisco.

Charlie filed for divorce several more times, always changing her mind at the last minute. Finally, in 1947, she divorced Ty after 39 years of marriage. In the divorce suit, she charged Ty with "extreme cruelty from the date of marriage to the present time." Charlie's brothers have said that Ty often beat Charlie, sometimes with a baseball bat. Charlie herself made no such claims. Given what we know about Cobb's temperament, however, it would not be surprising.

Cobb was delighted in 1936 to be first among the initial inductees elected to the new Baseball Hall of Fame. In his eyes, receiving the most votes proved what he had always felt. He was the greatest baseball player who ever lived.

For the most part, his life after baseball was very sad. He spent his time hunting, fishing, golfing, and traveling. He also spent a good deal of time doing business and trading stocks and bonds.

He was very lonely. Without baseball, his life felt empty. He began to smoke and to drink heavily. His temper and rages continued and, in fact, worsened, fueled by loneliness and alcohol. Stories appeared in California that he had punched a heckler in a nightclub. That he pushed a businessman into a fish pond. He even went to jail for abusing a police officer.

He tried marriage a second time. In 1949, at the age of 62, he married 40-year-old Frances Fairburn. "I'm just a lonely old man, sitting around a big, empty house," he told reporters. Seven years later, the couple divorced. Once again, Cobb was charged with "extreme cruelty." According to Frances, he was impossible to get along with when he was drunk.

Newly divorced, with two of his three sons dead (Herschel died of a heart attack in 1951), Cobb was almost totally alone. He began to donate some of his vast wealth. He built a hospital in his parents' name in his hometown of Royston, Georgia. He also established the Cobb Educational Fund. It awarded scholarships to underprivileged Georgia students going to college.

As his health began to fail, Cobb became concerned about his place in history. He attended as many "old-timer" games, dinners, and award banquets as he could. He needed to hear the applause of baseball fans. He needed to know that he was still remembered as one of the greats.

He also worked with two writers, John McCallum and Al Stump. He wanted to get his story out to the public. McCallum's 1956 book was a combination of biography and how-to, though it was filled with half-truths and misinformation. With Stump, he wrote an autobiography that was published shortly after his death. Later, Stump wrote his own biography of Cobb.

In 1959, Ty Cobb was diagnosed with cancer. For the next two years, he traveled the country. He visited casinos, hospitals, bars, and spring-training camps. Drinking heavily and heavily medicated, his tempers and furies never stopped.

He fought with everyone. For months, he had lived in a mansion without lights, heat, or hot water. The utility company had charged him an extra $16 that he would not pay. The company cut off his power. Rather than pay the $16, he sued the company. Waiting months for the case to be resolved, he took cold showers and lived by candlelight.

On June 5, 1961, he checked himself into Emory University Hospital in Atlanta. He carried with him a brown paper bag filled with $1 million worth of stocks, bonds, and securities. He also brought a loaded Lugar pistol.

Ty Cobb died on July 17, 1961. Before he died, his former wife, Charlie, his son Jimmy, and other family members visited him one last time.

Two Little Leaguers paid tribute to Ty Cobb on July 19, 1961, at his tomb in Royston, Georgia. Cobb had died two days earlier at the age of 74. Only three former major-league players attended his funeral.

His funeral was attended by close family members, Little League players from Royston, and three former big-league players. No other baseball players and no representatives from Major League Baseball came to say good-bye to Ty Cobb.

It is sad that so few people attended Cobb's funeral to show their respects. After all, he was probably the greatest baseball player who ever lived. His accomplishments as an athlete will live forever.

Al Stump once asked Cobb, "Why did you fight so hard in baseball, Ty?" Cobb answered, furiously, "I did it for my father, who was an exalted man. They killed him when he was still young. They blew his head off the same week I became a major leaguer. He never got to see me play. Not one game, not an inning. But I knew he was watching me . . . and I never let him down. *Never.*"

As a baseball player he never did let his father down. William Cobb would have had no reason to regret his decision to allow his son to follow his dream and play baseball.

Unfortunately, his accomplishments as a man off the field will live forever as well. Whatever it was that drove Ty Cobb to his rages and furies will never truly be known. Because of his behavior as a man, he died sad and alone. And that, for a man whose greatness as an athlete should have had the whole world mourning his loss, is very sad indeed.

TY COBB
Primary position: Center field

Full name: Tyrus Raymond Cobb •
Born: December 18, 1886, Banks County,
Georgia • Died: July 17, 1961, Atlanta,
Georgia • Height: 6'1" • Weight: 175 lbs.
• Teams: Detroit Tigers (1905–1926);
Philadelphia Athletics (1927–1928)

★ ★ ★ ★ ★ ★

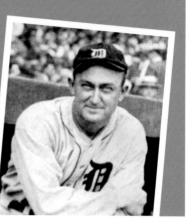

YEAR	TEAM	G	AB	H	HR	RBI	BA
1905	DET	41	150	36	1	15	.240
1906	DET	98	350	112	1	34	.320
1907	DET	150	605	212	5	119	.350
1908	DET	150	581	188	4	108	.324
1909	DET	156	573	216	9	107	.377
1910	DET	140	509	196	8	91	.385
1911	DET	146	591	248	8	127	.420
1912	DET	140	553	227	7	83	.410
1913	DET	122	428	167	4	67	.390
1914	DET	98	345	127	2	57	.368
1915	DET	156	563	208	3	99	.369
1916	DET	145	542	201	5	68	.371
1917	DET	152	588	225	6	102	.383
1918	DET	111	421	161	3	64	.382
1919	DET	124	497	191	1	70	.384
1920	DET	112	428	143	2	63	.334

Key: DET = Detroit Tigers; PHA = Philadelphia Athletics; G = Games; AB = At-bats;
H = Hits; HR = Home runs; RBI = Runs batted in; BA = Batting average

★ ★ ★ ★ ★ ★

(continued)

YEAR	TEAM	G	AB	H	HR	RBI	BA
1921	DET	128	507	197	12	101	.389
1922	DET	137	526	211	4	99	.401
1923	DET	145	556	189	6	88	.340
1924	DET	155	625	211	4	79	.338
1925	DET	121	415	157	12	102	.378
1926	DET	79	233	79	4	62	.339
1927	PHA	134	490	175	5	93	.357
1928	PHA	95	353	114	1	40	.323
Totals		3,035	11,429	4,191	117	1,938	.367

Key: DET = Detroit Tigers; PHA = Philadelphia Athletics; G = Games; AB = At-bats; H = Hits; HR = Home runs; RBI = Runs batted in; BA = Batting average

CHRONOLOGY

1886   **December 18** Born in Banks County, Georgia.

1899   Begins to play baseball.

1902   Joins the semi-pro Royston Reds.

1904   Tries out for the minor-league Augusta Tourists; is cut after two games; after playing well with the semi-pro Anniston Steelers, is called back to play for the Tourists.

1905   **August 8** His father is fatally shot by his mother.

        August 19 Called up to the major leagues by the Detroit Tigers.

1906   **March 30** His mother is acquitted of voluntary manslaughter in the death of her husband.

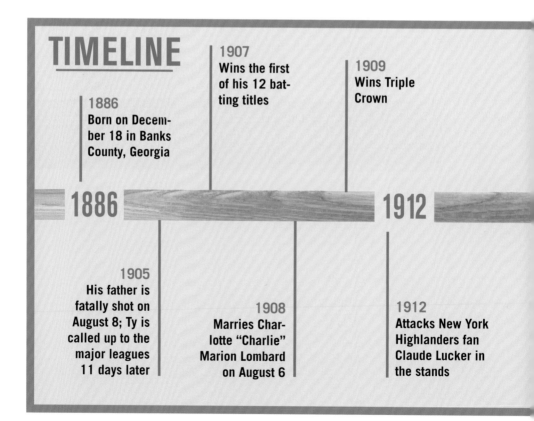

TIMELINE

1907
Wins the first of his 12 batting titles

1909
Wins Triple Crown

1886
Born on December 18 in Banks County, Georgia

1886

1912

1905
His father is fatally shot on August 8; Ty is called up to the major leagues 11 days later

1908
Marries Charlotte "Charlie" Marion Lombard on August 6

1912
Attacks New York Highlanders fan Claude Lucker in the stands

1907   Wins the first of his 12 batting titles.

Detroit Tigers win the American League championship; lose to the Chicago Cubs in the World Series.

1908   **August 6** Marries Charlotte "Charlie" Marion Lombard.

Detroit again loses to the Chicago Cubs in the World Series.

1909   Wins Triple Crown, leading the American League in batting average (.377), RBIs (107), and home runs (9).

Detroit loses the World Series to the Pittsburgh Pirates, four games to three.

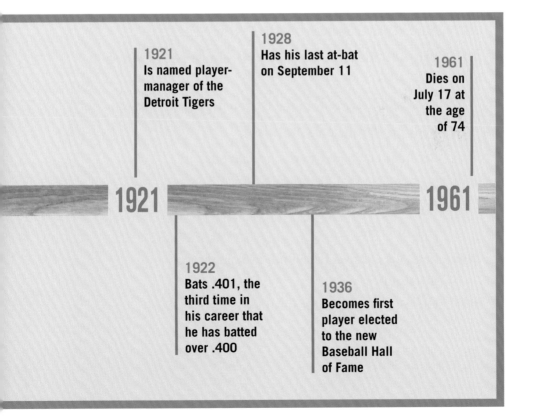

1921
Is named player-manager of the Detroit Tigers

1928
Has his last at-bat on September 11

1961
Dies on July 17 at the age of 74

1921   **1961**

1922
Bats .401, the third time in his career that he has batted over .400

1936
Becomes first player elected to the new Baseball Hall of Fame

1910 Wins controversial batting title over Napoleon Lajoie and receives a Chalmers automobile.

1911 Bats .420.

Wins Chalmers Award as American League's most valuable player.

1912 Attacks New York Highlanders fan Claude Lucker in the stands.

Bats .410 for sixth-straight batting title.

1915 Wins ninth-straight batting title.

1918 Serves three months in the U.S. Army's Chemical Warfare Service at the end of World War I.

1919 Hits .384 to win the American League batting title for his twelfth and final time.

1921 Named player-manager of the Detroit Tigers.

1922 Bats .401, the third time in his career that he has batted over .400.

1926 November 3 Resigns from the Detroit Tigers.

1927 Joins the Philadelphia Athletics.

Becomes first player to reach 4,000 hits.

1928 September 11 Has his last at-bat, ending a 24-year career.

1936 Becomes the first player elected to the new Baseball Hall of Fame.

1941 Beats his old rival Babe Ruth in a charity golf match-up.

1947 His wife, Charlie Cobb, divorces Ty after 39 years of marriage.

1961 July 17 Dies at the age of 74.

GLOSSARY

at-bat (AB)   An official turn at batting that is charged to a baseball player, except when the player walks, sacrifices, is hit by a pitched ball, or is interfered with by a catcher. At-bats are used to calculate a player's batting average and slugging percentage.

batting average   The number of hits a batter gets divided by the number of times the player is at bat. For example, 3 hits in 10 at-bats would be a .300 batting average.

bunt   A ball not fully hit, with the batter either intending to get to first base before the infielder can field the ball or allowing an existing base runner to advance.

curveball   A pitch that curves on its way to the plate, thanks to the spin a pitcher places on the ball when throwing. Also know as a "breaking ball."

the cycle   To hit for the cycle is to hit a single, a double, a triple, and a home run in the same game.

Dead Ball Era   The time period before the Lively Ball Era, when the structure of the baseball did not have the liveliness it has today. Most historians agree that the Dead Ball Era ended after the 1919 season.

double play   A play by the defense during which two offensive players are put out in a continuous action.

doubleheader   Two games played by the same two teams on the same day.

earned-run average (ERA)   The average number of runs a pitcher allows per nine-inning game; the runs must be scored without errors by defensive players.

emery ball   A baseball scuffed by an emery board.

error   The game's scorer designates an error when a defensive player makes a mistake that results in a runner reaching base or advancing a base.

fielding percentage   A statistic that reflects the percentage of times a defensive player successfully handles a batted or thrown ball. It is calculated by the sum of putouts and assists divided by the number of total chances.

hit-and-run   An offensive tactic in which a base runner (usually on first base) starts to run as if to steal and the batter is obligated to swing at the pitch.

line drive   A batted ball that is hit hard and has a low arc.

runs batted in (RBI)   The number of runs that score as a direct result of a batter's hit(s) are the runs batted in by that batter. The major-league record is 191 RBIs for a single season by one batter.

sacrifice   A ball hit by the batter that advances the runner to the next base while the batter receives an "out" for his attempt. Examples include a sacrifice fly and a sacrifice bunt.

slugging percentage   The number of bases a player reaches divided by the number of at-bats. It is a measure of the power of a batter.

spitball   A pitch that is altered by spit or some other substance. The pitch is more of a challenge to hitters since the ball moves differently because of changed wind resistance and weight on one side of the ball.

total bases   The sum of all the bases a hitter has accumulated. A single = 1; a double = 2; a triple = 3; a home run = 4.

Triple Crown   A player wins the Triple Crown when he leads the league in batting average, home runs, and runs batted in during a season.

BIBLIOGRAPHY

Alexander, Charles C. *Ty Cobb*. New York: Oxford University Press, 1984.

Bak, Richard. *Ty Cobb: His Tumultuous Life and Times*. Dallas: Taylor Publishing Group, 1994.

Cobb, Ty (with Al Stump). *My Life in Baseball: The True Record*. New York: Doubleday, 1961.

Rice, Grantland. *The Tumult and the Shouting: My Life in Sport*. New York: A.S. Barnes and Company, 1954.

Stump, Al. *Cobb: A Biography*. Chapel Hill, N.C.: Algonquin Books of Chapel Hill, 1994.

WEB SITES

Wikipedia: "Baseball Glove"

http://en.wikipedia.org/wiki/Baseball_glove

Wikipedia: "National Baseball Hall of Fame and Museum"

http://en.wikipedia.org/wiki/Baseball_hall_of_fame

Wikipedia: "Ty Cobb"

http://en.wikipedia.org/wiki/Ty_Cobb

FURTHER READING

Bak, Richard. *Peach: Ty Cobb in His Time and Ours.* Ann Arbor, Mich.: Sports Media Group, 2005.

Burns, Ken. *Baseball: An Illustrated History.* New York: Knopf, 1994.

Gutman, Dan. *Baseball's Biggest Bloopers: The Games That Got Away.* New York: Puffin Books, 1995.

Jacobs, William Jay. *They Shaped the Game: Ty Cobb, Babe Ruth, and Jackie Robinson.* New York: Atheneum, 1994.

Okkonen, Marc. *The Ty Cobb Scrapbook: An Illustrated Chronology of Significant Dates in the 24-Year Career of the Fabled Georgia Peach.* New York: Sterling Publishing Co., 2001.

Ritter, Lawrence S. *The Glory of Their Times: The Story of the Early Days of Baseball Told by the Men Who Played It.* New York: Vintage Books, 1985.

WEB SITES

Baseball Almanac

http://www.baseball-almanac.com

Baseball Reference

http://www.baseball-reference.com

MLB.com

http://mlb.mlb.com/index.jsp

National Baseball Hall of Fame and Museum

http://www.baseballhalloffame.org

The Official Web site of Ty Cobb

http://www.cmgworldwide.com/baseball/cobb/index.html

The Ty Cobb Museum

http://www.tycobbmuseum.org

PICTURE CREDITS

INDEX

ABOUT THE AUTHOR

DENNIS ABRAMS is the author of several books for Chelsea House, including biographies of Barbara Park, Anthony Horowitz, Hamid Karzai, and Viktor Yushchenko. He attended Antioch College, where he majored in English and communications. A voracious reader since the age of 3, Abrams lives in Houston, Texas, with his partner of 19 years, along with their two dogs and three cats.